CORAL REEFS

OF FLORIDA

CORAL REEFS
OF FLORIDA

GILBERT L. VOSS

PINEAPPLE PRESS 🍍 SARASOTA, FLORIDA

Library of Congress Cataloging-in-Publication Data

Voss. Gilbert L., 1918–
    Coral reefs of Florida / Gilbert L. Voss.
        p.   cm.
    Bibliography: p. 69
    Includes index.
    ISBN 0-910923-56-6 $14.95   ISBN 0-910923-57-4 (pbk.) $9.95
    1. Coral reef biology—Florida.   2. Coral reefs and islands—
Florida.   I. Title.
QH105.F6V67   1988
508.759—dc 19   88-9946
                                                                               CIP

First Edition
10 9 8 7 6 5 4 3 2 1

Design by Joan Lange Kresek
Typography by Birmy Graphics, Miami, Florida
Printed in Singapore through Palace Press

This book is dedicated to all those people who love the reefs and who have worked so hard to learn about them and to save them.

ACKNOWLEDGMENTS

So many people have helped in the writing of this book that it is impossible to mention them all. It originated with Marjory Stoneman Douglas who first asked me to write it, made many suggestions and critically reviewed the manuscript. Maureen Harwitz and Dagney Johnson provided insights into the politics involved in North Key Largo. Lt. Michael White, Superintendent of the Key Largo National Marine Sanctuary, Lt. Billy Causey, Superintendent of the Looe Key National Marine Sanctuary, and Dr. Renate Skinner, biologist of the John Pennekamp Coral Reef State Park, furnished much information and data on their respective areas and provided many of the color photographs. Drs. Donald de Sylva, Peter Glynn, Donald Moore and Samuel Snedaker of the Rosenstiel School of Marine and Atmospheric Science, University of Miami, read all or parts of the manuscript. Dr. James Bohnsack, National Marine Fisheries Service, read the manuscript and offered valuable suggestions. Others who read the manuscript in whole or in part and offered suggestions are Maureen Harwitz, Dagney Johnson and Lt. White. Drs. Eugene Shinn and Harold Hudson, U. S. Geological Survey, provided much information on coral growth and problems of the reefs. Harold Hudson also provided the x-radiograph of the coral. Dr. Charles Messing made the artwork for the text figures. To all of these people and others too numerous to mention, I extend my sincere thanks. Any errors that may occur are my own.

CONTENTS

FOREWORD

Innumerable people around the world are aware of the existence of corals and coral reefs. The very word coral triggers the imagination and evokes the romance that we all attach to the tropic seas. And yet the nature of the coral polyp itself and the multitudinous life of the reefs are practically unknown even to people most interested in the sea's marvels.

The very underwater life of the coral makes it a region of mystery. The many people who do not know about coral reefs will find in this small book a world almost completely unknown because it is hidden by the covering waters.

This book is a remarkable presentation of the life of corals which depend for their existence on the surrounding lagoon and terrestrial biota, geology and geography of the tropic world.

We are now aware that this wonderful region is being desperately threatened by the greatest predator of all—mankind. The encroachments, pollution and infinite damage worked by the human species now overrunning the shores of the tropical oceans is of the greatest possible concern to thousands of people. Yet, these interested thousands are largely ignorant of the true nature of this irreplaceable natural feature.

Because it is below the surface of the oceans, it is hidden from so many who do not have personal experience and observation of it, and thus have not been able to understand its workings and complex nature.

Among the scientists who know this vast area and are deeply concerned for its future are the marine scientists whose lives have been given over to this fascinating study. Among those are the scientists of the Rosenstiel School of Marine and Atmospheric Science of the University of Miami, situated with its laboratories and oceangoing research vessels on Virginia Key, on Biscayne Bay in Miami, Florida. And of these, few are more able or articulate than Dr. Gilbert Voss, who is a Professor of Biological Oceanography. It is tremendously gratifying that Dr. Voss has written this book, which we are sure will prove invaluable.

Dr. Voss has published over 130 scientific and popular papers and books on marine and terrestrial life of Florida and the Caribbean. He has been active for over 30 years in the study of problems of tropical and subtropical environments from hardwood hammocks to shallow bays and estuaries and coral reefs. He had the foresight in 1957 to take the first important steps to protect the Key Largo reef tract by proposing the establishment of the John Pennekamp Coral Reef State Park and he proposed the original regulations for the park.

He was the Principal Investigator on a two-year National Oceanographic and Atmospheric Administration (NOAA) baseline study to determine the characteristics, species diversity and communities of the coral reefs, hard bottom, sand and grass zones within the Sanctuary. He demonstrates the importance of the efforts of a single individual who determines that there is a problem, and who dedicates his time and energy to solve the problem.

We are delighted that Pineapple Press saw the great value of Dr. Voss' work and we are proud that we have been able to support his presentation. We owe a special debt of gratitude to the Garden Group of Ocean Reef, Key Largo, for their support of this book.

It is the concern of every forward-looking citizen that our lives are completely conditioned by the environment in which we live. Everyone of us must feel responsibility toward the safeguarding of the future.

Marjory Stoneman Douglas
Coconut Grove
January, 1988

CORAL REEFS

OF FLORIDA

INTRODUCTION

Running slowly out from shore across the Hawk Channel the boat seems suspended in space. Without a ripple on the surface, water and air seem one, the bottom passing beneath the bow with startling clarity. In the early morning light the boat casts long shadows on the bottom, momentarily scaring fish from their early breakfast in the turtle grass.

The approaching reef first appears yellowish in the green waters of the lagoon but then turns to yellows, browns and purple as the boat cruises over the living reef. Multicolored fish swim slowly aside. Waving sea fans and plumes seem to reach upward to impede the passage of the boat. Suddenly great coral heads loom upward, elkhorn coral nearly breaking the surface. Vase sponges offer up their catch of shells and pebbles.

Offshore, a school of bottlenose dolphins breaks the surface, their sleek bodies appearing momentarily, then sliding downward, leaving hardly a ripple. To starboard a houndfish flees in long leaps, and a flyingfish, barely holding itself in flight in the still air, skitters over the surface propelled by the rapid beating of its tail.

As you cross over the reef, the water deepens, displaying coral caverns and surge channels. Then suddenly the bottom drops away into the deep blue waters of the Straits of Florida.

The boat is turned back to the reef, the anchor is dropped and you slip over the side into the cool embracing water. Through your face mask the bottom is visible as if you were looking through a window into a marine garden. You feel suspended in midair. With a kick of your flippers you descend into this fairy world of motion, the brightly colored fishes moving slowly aside from your path as you swim among the corals and waving sea plumes. It is a world of enchantment, completely foreign to the land dweller.

As you swim about, a dull rhythmic thumping hits your ears. You surface to locate the source of this alien sound and there, just outside the reef, an oil tanker is gliding by, forefoot out of water, the propeller blades chunking with each revolution. You watch her as she passes, her bow throwing a curving green wave. The wave comes across the reef, rocks your boat briefly, and passes shoreward across the lagoon. Only the swaying sea fans mark her passage. You dive again and again and as the day comes alive, a breath of wind stirs, the surface of the sea ripples as it passes, and the spell is broken. You are in the water, the air and sea meet, the illusion of floating in the sea-air is lost. You are an intruder in a watery world.

This is the way to first encounter the coral reef and to feel its mystery and enchantment. The coral reefs of Florida have entranced and captured humans from the first visitor to the Florida reefs encased in Spanish mail armor, to more recent ones in wet suits or bikinis.

The great coral reefs of the Florida Keys are the only true coral reefs in the continental waters of the United States. The Florida reef tract, composed of outer reefs and patch reefs, contains over 50 species of corals comprising over 80 percent of all coral reef species in the tropical western Atlantic. Unique among the reefs of the world, the Florida and Caribbean reefs are covered by forests of waving sea plumes, whips and fans in constant motion so that the reef appears to be a living being. No reefs of the Pacific or Indian oceans resemble them in this respect.

Amongst the corals and plumes swim an amazing array of multicolored fishes—blue angels, tangs, queen triggers, parrotfishes, butterflyfishes, and hordes of others, often so tame that one can almost reach out and touch them. Spiny lobster antennae project beneath rocky ledges, the lobsters protected by the long, sharp spines of the ever-present black sea urchins. Giant helmet shells burrow about in the sandy back reef areas in search of sea biscuit urchins, while queen conchs jerk themselves along the grass beds in search of food.

In the background lurk the vicious-appearing barracudas with silvery sides and gaping jaws filled with razor sharp teeth, watching for passing prey. Caribbean reef squid, enquiring but wary, keep watch over the reef, warning other less alert animals of possible danger. Hawksbill turtles swim slowly along the grass beds and occasional nurse sharks swim by seeking succulent lobsters along the reef edge.

Today, the reefs may best be visited in the Biscayne National Park, the Pennekamp Coral Reef State Park or in the Key Largo and Looe Key National Marine Sanctuaries. So many people have become captivated by the reefs that in Pennekamp alone over 600,000 visits were made to the reef in 1986. The reefs are one of the major attractions of Florida and the nation. Florida is the number one diving destination in the world with ten times the number of visitors of the second highest rated diving area, Australia. Visitors come in sail and power boats, diving boats and glass-bottom tour boats. So many come that the reefs are in danger of being destroyed by the sheer numbers of visitors.

The attraction of the reefs has its perils, for it affords land developers

a major selling point for entranced buyers for as yet unconstructed condominiums with marinas and boat basins, beckoning them to the reefs
offshore. But as the land is developed and the shoreline changed, subtle
and sometimes not so subtle changes occur in the bordering waters. The
very precious land and the tropical enchantment of the keys and the reefs
are themselves slowly but inexorably leading to the demise of the lagoon
and the coral reefs. Few people realize the tragic picture unfolding in this
unique underwater sanctuary.

It is with the hope that the public and especially the visitors to the
coral reefs may become aware of these dangers to this last frontier that
this book has been written. It can tell you of the dangers confronting the
ecosystem of the keys, the lagoon and the reefs, but only a dive amongst
the life of the reef can truly bring home the imminent disaster to this
unique habitat.

1
FLORIDA'S CORAL REEFS

The Florida Keys extend in a long, curving line like beads in a necklace from Fowey Rock near Miami to the little cluster of islands forming the Dry Tortugas about 65 miles west of Key West (Figure 1). With their rich tropical vegetation and dark-leaved mangroves, they appear like emeralds lying in a turquoise sea. They are low islands, rising only a few feet above sea level, apparently susceptible to being swept away by the first tropical hurricane roaring its way up out of the Caribbean. Battered by towering seas and hurricane force winds, the keys would seem doomed. But they are protected on the west by the mainland and the shallow waters of Florida Bay and to the east and south by the coral reefs and the shallow lagoon.

The coral reefs seem unlikely protectors. Composed of fragile limestone built up over thousands of years by billions of tiny soft-bodied animals, the coral polyps, they too are likely victims of hurricane seas. Battered by the tremendous force of the crashing surf, huge coral heads may be torn off and hurled across the bottom for hundreds of yards. The more fragile branching species may be flattened and crushed, looking like rubble after a battle. But when the storm subsides, the little polyps continue reproducing, multiplying, growing, until in a few years the damage has been repaired and reef life goes on. And the keys still stand behind them. There are well over 100 coral reefs spread along the seaward side of the keys from Fowey Rocks to the Dry Tortugas. Their names have the ring

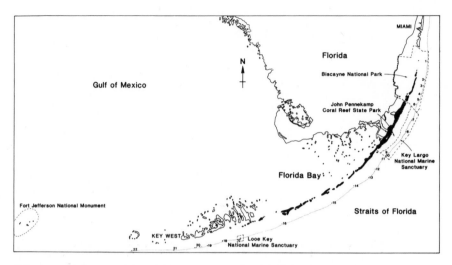

Figure 1. The Florida Keys with the state and national parks, sanctuaries and monuments. Black keys are formed of Key Largo Limestone, others of Miami Oolite. Numbers indicate reefs: 1. Fowey Rocks, 2. Triumph, 3. Long, 4. Ajax, 5. Pacific, 6. Elkhorn, 7. Carysfort, 8. The Elbow, 9. French, 10. Molasses, 11. Pickles, 12. Conch, 13. Crocker, 14. Alligator, 15. Tennessee, 16. Sombrero Key, 17. Looe Key, 18. American Shoal, 19. Pelican Shoal, 20. The Sambos, 21. Sand Key, 22. Cosgrove.

of romance and mystery: Long Reef, Ajax, Triumph, Tennessee, Alligator, the Sambos, Carysfort, Molasses, French, Crocker's, Hen and Chickens, Turtle Rocks, Key Largo Dry Rocks, Sombrero, American Shoal, Looe Key. Many of them are named for ships that have gone ashore in storms, their bottoms ripped open by the jagged corals lying like fangs below the surface of the sea.

Inshore, beyond the placid waters of the lagoon, lie the keys, strung in a line, lying on the remains of old coral reefs. There are many keys, some still with their hardwood hammocks composed of gumbo limbo, mahogany, ironwood, mastic, stoppers, poisonwood, paradise trees, all names strange to Northern ears. Others are covered with red, white and black mangroves, while here and there are larger keys with stands of Caribbean pines and the immigrant Australian pine or beefwood.

The northernmost keys are sandy barrier islands such as Key Biscayne, but these are followed by the true keys from little Soldier Key to giant Key Largo, the Matecumbes, Key West and the Dry Tortugas.

The Florida Keys are gifts from the sea, their coral rock foundations built by the work of billions of tiny soft-bodied coral polyps extracting

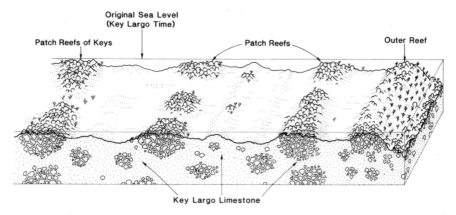

Figure 2. Block diagram indicating reefs and sea level across the reef tract in Key Largo time. (after Hoffmeister, 1974)

calcium from the sea that bathes them and depositing it in thin layers to form their stony calcareous skeletons.

About 100,000 years ago the sea level was about 25 feet higher than now and much of Florida was under water. Sea action eroded away the land and formed a wide plateau only a few feet below the sea. In this shallow Pamlico Sea two types of bottom were formed, Miami oolite made up of little calcareous spheres (ooids) and bryozoans or moss animals, and Key Largo Limestone formed from the corals of the patch and outer reefs, the foundation matrix of the Upper Keys (Figure 2).

During the glacial period, when the sea level dropped by more than 150 feet and the shallow platform or terrace was exposed to air, rain, and surf, the coral reefs died and were cemented together to form coral rock. When the level of the sea rose again in our present interglacial period, the corals spread out over the Key Largo Limestone rock wherever it was exposed above the soft sediments and began to grow upward again to form our present reefs (Figure 3).

Thus the Key Largo Limestone shows distributions that mirror the corals living above them except for the line of Pleistocene reef that now forms the keys themselves. Only in the Upper Keys and especially off Key Largo do ancient reefs and living corals show a common origin and continuous history.

When the inner line of reef became dry rock, floating debris began to accumulate on it and slowly became covered with a thin layer of soil,

FLORIDA'S CORAL REEFS   19

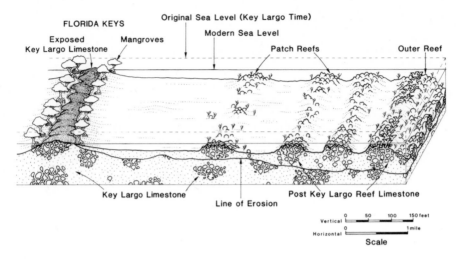

Figure 3. Block diagram indicating reefs and sea level across the reef tract at present. (after Hoffmeister, 1974)

deeper where it lodged in erosion basins or pits. With the accumulation of organic materials plants and trees took root, the seeds carried to the developing keys by ocean currents sweeping upward out of the Caribbean.

The vegetation bore little resemblance to that of the rest of the Floridian Plateau for it was tropical, the child of the hardwood forests of the Yucatan Peninsula, Honduras, Nicaragua, northern South America and the islands of the Antillean Arc, Hispaniola and Cuba.

Along with the hardwood forests that now are the hammocks of the keys came mangroves, tree snails with their gaudy shells, white-crowned pigeons, Caribbean landcrabs, tropical orchids and many others to take up their abode.

In the shallow grass flats and among the coral reefs came myriads of marine animals from snails to fish, corals to worms, colorful crabs and waving sea plumes, all from the tropical waters and found nowhere else in the waters of the peninsula.

The first people to inhabit the keys were the early pre-Colombian Indians, perhaps Tequestas like the Indians from around Biscayne Bay. They were well established on the keys as is shown by the various kitchen middens and shell artifacts still to be seen on Key Largo and other keys.

Juan Ponce de Leon coasted the keys when he first discovered Florida for Spain. Watching the keys from beyond the reef he thought that they looked like a line of people and called them Los Martires, the martyrs. Menendez coasted them on his way from St. Augustine to Havana and the courier route between these two towns lay behind the reefs as far as Cayo Hueso or Bone Key, now Key West. Later the reefs became the lurking place of pirates who preyed upon passing ships. Among these pirates may have been Black Caesar, who reputedly holed up at Caesar's Creek.

Later, Cuban fishermen established a small settlement at Key West, soon to be surrounded by the shore buildings of the United States Navy, sent in 1822 to wipe out the pirate scourge. Under the able direction of Commodore Porter, operations began immediately and successfully.

With the elimination of the pirates, shipping increased—only to find that the coral reefs were even more dangerous. Wreckers from the Bahamas came over to ply their trade in saving lives and cargoes. Their headquarters were at Tavernier and Indian Key, with salvage taken to be adjudicated in the federal court at Key West.

However, so many ships were lost on the Florida reefs that it was decided that a series of lighthouses should be erected on them and in 1851 the Coast Survey sent the ship *Bibb* to survey the reefs. Aboard was the Swiss biologist, Louis Agassiz, who made a biological study of the coral reefs, the first scientific study of the reefs and the keys.

More people followed the shipping business and the profitable fishing offered by the reefs. Farming began and plantations were developed, the largest ones being on Key Largo.

The sunshine, cool ocean breezes, temperate climate and the enchantment of the reefs and their surrounding waters made the keys a retreat and a cure for invalids from the North. Sport fishermen began to arrive to fish for sailfish, tarpon and the lightning swift bonefish.

But man, in his insatiable greed and search for wealth, is rapidly destroying the keys, their vegetation and that which lives beneath the sea and gave it birth. The keys belong to the sea but the sea has been ignored. What the sea has given, if mistreated by man, it can take away, as inevitably as is now occurring in this once tropical paradise. To protect the land, the shallow seas, and the coral reefs, one must understand them. It all starts with the coral polyps—tiny, defenseless, ignored, laboring upwards against increasing odds, not the least of which is man.

2

CORALS AND CORAL REEFS

Corals are coelenterates, the large phylum or group of animals that includes the jellyfishes, sea anemones, sea feathers, whips and fans, hydroids and soft corals. The stony corals or scleractinians that form the backbone of the coral reefs are distinguished from the other members of the phylum by their hard, calcareous skeletons composed of thin plates or layers of calcium carbonate secreted by the soft coral polyp, the living animal.

Each individual coral polyp has the appearance of a tiny sea anemone, its base attached to its little limy cup (Figure 4). But the polyp's sides and base are infolded in sometimes intricate designs resulting in a cup of calcium carbonate that displays ridges or septa with different patterns for each species. The cups holding the polyp grow upward over time, and if these can be followed, their growth lines can provide a time and growth scale for the coral. If a coral head is broken off, taken into the laboratory and sliced into thin sheets with a diamond saw, the skeleton can then be X-rayed and the past growth history shown by the annular rings of the coral. These rings can be correlated with time, like tree rings, giving the growth rate and age of the coral.

Corals reproduce both sexually and asexually. In sexual reproduction the coral produces eggs and sperm on the swollen edges of the divisions or mesenteries within the polyp's body. In many corals, when the polyps are mature or in spawning condition, the sperm are released through the

23

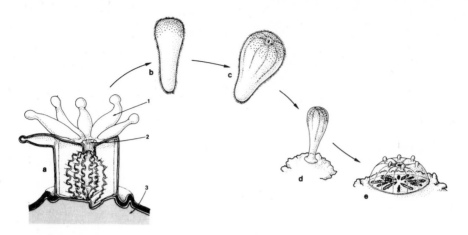

Figure 4. Life cycle of a stony coral. a. coral polyp: 1. tentacle, 2. mouth, 3. hard skeleton, b. newly ejected planula, c. planula beginning development, d. planula attached to bottom, e. newly developing polyp. (after Hoffmeister, 1974 and Duerden, 1904)

mouth of the polyp and are carried by water currents to other polyps where the sperm fertilize the eggs still attached to the mesenteries.

After development, the eggs are released and pass out through the mouth of the parent polyp. The free-swimming larva, the planula, looks much like a tiny pear and is about the size of a pin head, covered with rapidly beating hairs or cilia. It may remain swimming for two or three weeks, after which the planula settles to the bottom and attaches at one end to a suitable hard substrate. The free end forms a cuplike depression surrounded by tentacle buds. The cup develops into a cavity with a mouth opening and becomes a small coral polyp. It now begins to precipitate lime to form a cup-shaped home and the beginning of a new coral colony.

As the coral polyp grows upward, it may reproduce asexually by budding off a new polyp which in turn buds off another, each with its calcareous cup. This budding process and skeletal construction goes on until in this way the final coral, as we know it, is formed. If growth is mainly lateral and upward, the resulting colony may form one of the massive coral heads. If growth and polyp formation is mainly terminal, the resulting colony will be one of the branched type. Not all corals form colonies, however. Some, such as the Pacific *Fungia* are single coral polyps. Solitary corals, as they are called, are numerous in the Pacific Ocean. Most deep-sea corals are solitary and small.

Another form of asexual reproduction is multiplication by fragmentation. If a living coral colony is broken apart or fragmented by storms or by boat groundings, some of the coral fragments may, if undisturbed and in favorable conditions, grow into new corals firmly attached to the bottom. But many broken fragments are killed by micropredators such as worms, gastropod mollusks and others.

On reefs with heavy surf, this may be a common method of forming new colonies and increasing the size of the reef. Unfortunately, much of the breaking up of the corals by boat damage results in the death of the fragments from wave movement and lack of proper growing conditions.

During the day, the tentacles of the coral polyps are withdrawn and the polyps are inactive. At night, the normal feeding time of most corals, the tentacles are expanded, waving slowly about in the water to capture small plankton, floating organic material and even small fish. The tentacles possess stinging cells or nematocysts with tiny darts and a weak poison, sufficient to kill their prey. These darts are shot out on contact with prey and paralyze it, after which the prey is drawn into the mouth and digested in the body cavity.

The rate of growth of corals and coral reefs has been the subject of much study. By the sectioning and X-ray technique described previously, one can study various species that make up the coral reef matrix and as a result determine the rate of growth of the reefs. Studies done in Florida indicate that the massive corals such as *Montastrea* grow at a rate of about half an inch or less each year. On the other hand, corals that grow by the extension of their branch tips, such as the staghorn coral *Acropora cervicornis,* may grow as much as four inches a year.

Stony corals are divided into two groups or types, the hermatypic corals that form the shallow reefs of the tropics and the ahermatypic corals that occur more commonly in cold waters and the deep sea. Reef-building or hermatypic corals contain within their body tissues minute algae known as zooxanthellae. These single-celled plants take up carbon dioxide, a waste product of the coral polyp, and, by photosynthesis in the presence of sunlight, give off oxygen that is used by the polyp. In addition to providing oxygen, the zooxanthellae act as a catalyst, aiding in the production of calcium carbonate and thus assisting in coral skeletal growth. Another important role of zooxanthellae involves translocation of sugar, amino acids and other nutrients. It is only with the assistance of the zooxanthellae that the reef corals are able to grow their massive skeletons and maintain themselves at a level just below the sea surface, growing upward as sea level rises.

The environmental factors controlling the growth and well-being of corals are primarily full strength seawater with a salinity of around 35 parts per thousand of salts to water, water temperatures between 20 and 30 degrees Celsius (68 to 86 degrees Fahrenheit), water clarity sufficient to permit their zooxanthellae to photosynthesize, and an adequate food supply. Because of lower temperature and reduced water clarity, reef-building corals do not occur north of Fowey Rocks just south of Miami. North of there water turbidity is increased because of sediments in suspension in the water. The average water clarity in the Florida Keys, without interference from humans, is sufficient to permit natural growth rates. Water turbidity is increased during storms that bring the fine calcium carbonate sediments into suspension in the shallow waters. During calm weather these sediments settle to the bottom and the water is clear. Heavy boat traffic with propellers disturbing the sediments, dredging and land filling—all cause long-term water turbidity.

Increasing turbidity and resulting decreasing water clarity reduce coral growth by inhibiting the action of the zooxanthellae. A coral sectioned for analysis of growth showed that the coral had nearly ceased its growth during the period in the keys when dredge and fill operations were at their peak but regained its normal growth after the moratorium on dredge and fill went into effect, showing dramatically the effect that decreased water quality has on coral growth (Figure 5).

Another cause of turbidity and thus lowered water clarity is eutrophication or an overload of nutrients resulting in heavy phytoplankton blooms. When eutrophication is present, the water is yellowish green from the presence of masses of minute algae. Eutrophication can reduce water clarity so much that both coral and seagrass growth is inhibited. Eutrophication can be caused by rain runoff loaded with fertilizers or sewage outflow or seepage.

As a result of the above factors, coral growth is inhibited along much of the Florida coast. Coral reefs are limited in the western Atlantic from about 30 degrees north latitude to 30 degrees south latitude. Along the North American coast coral reefs are found only along the east coast of Florida from the Dry Tortugas to just south of Miami at Fowey Rocks. Because of cooler water temperatures and reduced water clarity reefs do not occur in the Gulf of Mexico, except for the Flower Gardens off the Texas coast, although individual coral heads are found as far north as Tampa and Cedar Key in somewhat deeper water, but they do not form reefs.

North of Miami corals are found as far as North Carolina on the shallow

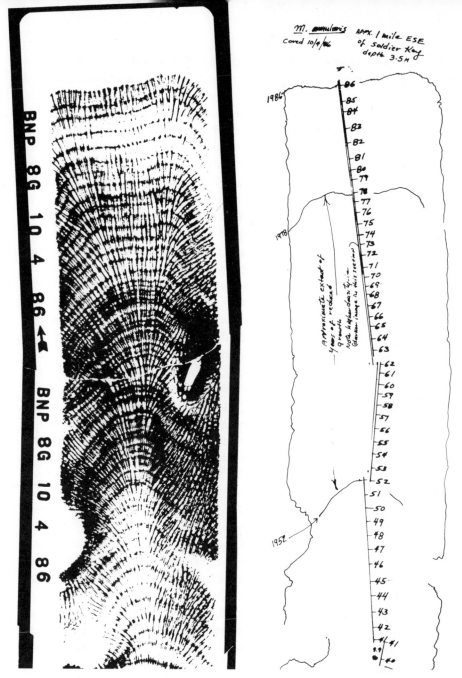

Figure 5. An X-radiograph of a section of *Montastrea annularis* from off Soldier Key showing annual growth rings from 1940 to 1986. Note greatly reduced growth from 1952 to 1978 while dredge and fill was active. Mode of budding off of new polyps can be seen by following individual polyp growth. (X-radiograph by Dr. Harold Hudson, U. S. Geological Survey)

CORALS AND CORAL REEFS 27

shelf near the warm waters of the Gulf Stream but only as single colonies and not as reefs that grow upward to the surface. The northernmost record of coral reefs in the western North Atlantic is at Bermuda where the corals are bathed by the warm waters of the Gulf Stream and the Sargasso Sea.

Coral reefs in the United States mainland reach their greatest development off the Florida Keys and primarily in the northern keys off Key Largo. Their high development there is probably because the reefs are sheltered from the waters of Florida Bay which pour into the Straits through numerous passages between the keys. In the winter, because of its shoal depths, the waters of Florida Bay may become so cold and turbid from winter cold fronts that they may inhibit coral growth. The protection provided by Key Largo has permitted the coral reefs to reach the peak of their development in the Pennekamp Coral Reef State Park and the Key Largo National Marine Sanctuary.

A typical coral reef is formed where corals can grow luxuriantly into large colonies. As the corals grow larger and larger, they become crowded together. New corals grow between them, helping to fill the reef with coral skeletons. In the crevices and cracks between the corals a large variety of calcareous fragments of many kinds help to fill in the free spaces. These are small pieces of coral, shell fragments, sponge spicules, the calcareous sclerites of horny corals, algal plates, foraminiferan skeletons and many others. These are slowly cemented together by chemical means and by the growth of the coralline algae, such as *Lithothamnion* and its relatives. Thus, through many different means, the calcareous mixture of corals and reef dwellers of other kinds are bound into the coral base rock of the reef with only the living corals and their associates on the outer surface. Further cementation can go on to form solid rock such as the Key Largo Limestone which was formed in this manner.

A typical outer or barrier reef of the Upper Keys is shown in Figure 6. The fore reef is composed of large coral heads such as *Montastrea*, which help to break the force of the surf, followed somewhat shallower on the reef by the elkhorn coral *Acropora palmata*. In some reefs, such as at Carysfort, there is a typical coralline algal ridge that forms a mammillated surface over the coral skeletons and is the upper surface that takes the brunt of the seas. Above this is the reef crest, formed of coral rubble on which are growing sea fans and whips, small colonies of corals, some sponges, and numerous calcareous green algae such as *Halimeda*, and low growths of brown algae. On the back of the reef the staghorn coral *Acropora cervicornis* is most prominent. Its broken-off, rodlike

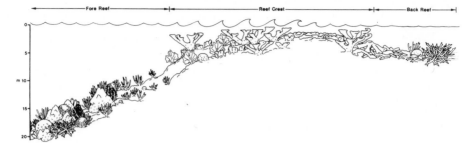

Figure 6. Cross section of a typical outer reef showing zonation. *Montastrea annularis* is common in fore reef, *Acropora palmata* in reef crest, with *Acropora cervicornis* in back reef.

pieces may form a major covering on the back portion of the reef crest. Here also may be found a number of other species of corals although less conspicuous. On some reefs, such as at Key Largo Dry Rocks and Ajax Reef, the fire coral *Millepora alcicornis*, not a true coral, is conspicuous on the fore reef.

Along the back edge of the reef crest, blades of the sea grass *Thalassia testudinum* begin to protrude from between the coral rubble. The blades become more and more numerous until the reef flat turns mainly into lush growths or meadows of turtle grass that finally form the meadows of the bottom of the lagoon and the Hawk Channel.

The lagoon or patch reefs show a different structure (Figure 7). Sheltered by the outer reef line and surrounded by water only about 15 to 20 feet deep, there is seldom a true fore reef and the massive coral heads rise directly from the bottom, growing along the sides of the old dead coral matrix. The corals grow upward to just below the surface of the sea

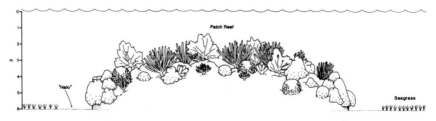

Figure 7. Cross section of a typical patch reef. Note clear space or "halo" around base of reef kept clear of turtle grass by the grazing of fish and sea urchins. Patch reefs are composed mainly of brain corals of various species and sea fans, plumes and whips.

CORALS AND CORAL REEFS   29

and the top of the reef is usually covered with staghorn coral interspersed with brain coral and with gorgonians covering the top. Unlike the outer reefs that have a solid matrix of coral skeletons, honeycombed with small caverns, gorges, and surge channels, the patch reefs may be nearly hollow inside, dissolved away by sea water. In some that have been investigated, once an opening has been made, one can stand within the cavern formed by the corals.

The environmental conditions for the growth of reef corals and for the formation of reefs are well known and have already been given. It is because of these environmental requirements that coral reefs are found mainly on the eastern side of continents and large islands along the course of the warm ocean curents. While corals and coral reefs are found on the west side of continents, they are usually concentrated in the equatorial regions and have a shorter north and south distribution. In the continental waters of the United States, coral reefs are found only along the Florida Keys. There are no shallow water coral reefs in the Gulf of Mexico in United States waters nor along the west coast of the United States where the water is either too cold or upwellings cause high turbidity preventing coral growth.

3

THE REEF COMMUNITY

While the visitor to the reef is at first impressed by the massiveness and configurations of the corals, their creamy to green or brown colors, and the majestic seascapes that they present, it is the other dwellers of the reefs that soon captivate one and bring out the camera. Most obvious and spectacular are the reef fishes, often gaudily colored, spotted, striped and barred, apparently unafraid of humans. These are followed by the blue, purple, greenish and yellow gorgonians or sea whips, plumes and fans. It is these that make diving on an Atlantic reef a unique experience, for they wave slowly about with the current and swell action until the whole reef seems alive, in constant motion. And indeed it is, from its coral matrix to the thousands of animals and plants that live around, on and in the reef and even in the coral themselves. It is this horde of life that makes up the reef community.

Most conspicuous of the reef fishes are the French angels, blue parrotfish, queen parrotfish, queen triggerfish and rock beauties on the outer reefs, while the commoner ones are the yellowtail snapper, French grunt, surgeonfish, sergeant major and blue tang. On the patch reefs among the commonest fishes are the white grunt, stoplight parrotfish, yellowtail snapper, bluehead, several damselfishes and the redband parrotfish.

The reefs afford a home for hundreds of thousands of specimens of over 150 species of tropical fish or over two-thirds of all of the species found within the Key Largo reef tract and its lagoon. Because of the hollow structure of some reefs, almost twice the number of fish occupy the reef than can be seen at any one time by a visitor. Indeed, the reef can be considered as a marine tenement house, but with a difference, for there is double occupancy, a night shift and a day shift. The fish that feed during the day either on the reef or on the grass meadows surrounding it come in at night to rest or sleep in the safety of the reef while those that occupied the reef during the day take their turn to feed at night, a system of "hot berthing."

Conspicuous around patch reefs and large coral heads or clumps is a circle of bare white coral sand or "halo" as it is called. This area is kept clear of sea grasses by the grazing of herbivorous fishes and the width of the halo is the distance that the fish feels safe for a quick retreat to the reef if a predator comes upon the scene. It is also caused by the grazing of the longspined black sea urchin.

Other herbivorous fishes are the parrotfishes that feed directly on the living coral, possibly to get the algae contained in their tissues and within the outer surface of the stony skeleton. The scars caused by the nibbling of the parrotfish are sometimes obvious to a knowledgeable swimmer but may not be recognized by the casual visitor.

The reefs are thus the home of many fishes of interest to the diver and to the sport and commercial fisherman. Without them, a major source of enjoyment and livelihood would be missing from the keys. But besides the fishes there are hosts of invertebrates that also make up the reef community. They are so numerous that only a few can be mentioned.

Under rocks and cemented onto the shells of reef mollusks are colonies of the single-celled, dark-red foraminiferan, usually smaller than a dime. Their calcareous skeletons on mollusk shells are an indicator that the mollusks came from a coral reef.

Sponges are everywhere, in a variety of shapes and colors. Mostly brownish or yellowish, they live between the corals attached to the coral basement. Red ones are often poisonous and if touched may give a sting that is painful and may persist for days. Many kinds of sponges are found coating the undersides of coral slabs, often a beautiful light blue or bright yellow or snow white. The larger sponges are filled with tubes and galleries occupied by tiny shrimps, sometimes thousands within a single loggerhead sponge. Other sponges may afford homes to sponge worms, small mollusks and other forms of life.

Other kinds of coelenterates than corals live on and within the reef. The gorgonians are often spectacular. Looking more like plants than living animals, they are formed of colonies of tiny polyps growing around a central stalk of horny material. Often imported from the Bahamas and sold in curio stores, they were once collected in great numbers in the Florida Keys but are now protected by state laws. They too offer homes to many kinds of animals including the gaudy flamingo tongue mollusks, basket starfish, and secretive, well-camouflaged grass shrimp. Sea anemones, many beautifully colored, are attached to the rocks or burrowed in the sand. When disturbed, they contract into shapeless blobs.

Allied to the corals are the fire or stinging corals of the reefs. They form stony skeletons, cream-colored, with tiny pores occupied by the minute polyps. The colonies may be upright, irregular plates or thin coatings over dead gorgonian skeletons forming almost fernlike stony colonies. The tiny polyps are armed with powerful stinging cells and the unwary swimmer who brushes against them will regret it for some time. When their larvae are released at spawning they may cause so-called "hot spots" that can severely sting divers who encounter them.

Marine worms or polychaetes are common. Most spectacular are those that form their calcareous tube homes in existing burrows in live coral heads. Each worm has a crown of brightly colored tentacles spread out in the water to entrap plankton. They are sensitive to light and contract instantly in the shadow of a swimmer. One species, called the Christmas tree worm, is a favorite of photographers.

Crawling about among the corals are large green or reddish, fuzzy, flattened worms, their sides fringed with soft white or pinkish bristles. These orange and green bristle worms are called fire worms as the soft, harmless-appearing bristles can give a painful sting, the effect of which can be felt for hours or days.

The coral reefs are swarming with shrimps and crabs. They live beneath coral slabs and rocks, in crevices and caves. They burrow down beneath the surface of the sand and rubble, live inside sponges and form galls in corals. They live under the reef edge and the faster ones live brazenly but hazardously crawling about over the reef rock. They are also noisy creatures, filling the reef with a myriad of clicks, snaps, crackles and rasping sounds. The "Silent World" indeed!

Spiny lobsters, or crawfish as the natives call them, disclose their presence by their long antennae projecting from beneath coral slabs. On the top of the reef among the algae the spray crab dodges would-be predators while a sponge, moving slowly across the bottom, reveals the camouflaged sponge crab carrying its concealment on its back. Small spiny and hairy crabs hide in the rubble and occasionally there is the beautiful rose and yellow coral crab, looking much like a stone crab except in color.

Snapping shrimp, each with its large pistol claw, hide in the algae or under rocks. On the purple sea plumes the long, slender, purple grass shrimp cling to the branches, invisible to the closest searcher until disturbed. If one finds a small rocky ledge, it may be a cleaning station, signalled by the long, waving antennae of a brightly colored shrimp attracting a fish to the station to have its parasites picked off and eaten. And in the turtle grass a sleek, green thumbsplitter or mantis shrimp glides through the grass, snakelike, its striking claws held tightly under its chest.

Although rare today, occasional triton shells are still found, feeding among the rocks. And queen or pink conchs live in the back reef. Under coral slabs are smooth, glossy cowrie shells or micrimocs, in life the shell covered by the knobby, soft mantle. Also under rocks may be cone shells, mottled golden brown, gray or white, with dartlike teeth that may be poisonous. Flamingo tongue shells with pale cream mantle with striking brown markings crawl about on gorgonians eating the polyps.

The Caribbean reef octopus hunts along the reef, searching for cowries and other mollusks. The Caribbean reef squid may patrol the reef, flashing warnings to the other reef denizens when danger approaches.

One of the most numerous groups of animals is the echinoderms. Long-spined black sea urchins dwell under the edges of old toppled coral heads or in the overhang of the reef. Their needle sharp spines will penetrate canvas shoes and even swim fins. Nearly every rock, when overturned, discloses the long, slender spiny-armed brittlestars. When exposed, they swim, crawl or twist and turn their way back into the refuge of holes and crevices. The basket star is often found wound around the branches of sea plumes, seemingly tied in a knot. But at night the arms are spread out and the branches form a network in the current to capture plankton. Besides these there are the comet stars whose irregularly shaped arms give this starfish its name. Sea cucumbers live among the corals and under rocks. They crawl about engulfing the sands, digesting out the organic material and excreting the sand, now made finer by mechanical grinding and digestive juices. They turn over thousands of tons of bottom sediments annually in and around the reefs and thus contribute to the fine sands of the reef and the reef flat.

Besides these obvious animals, there are many much smaller ones that live beneath the old coral rock and coat their under surface with mats of varying hues. These include bryozoans or moss animals and beautiful encrusting sponges varying in color from red to bright yellow or heavenly blue. Amidst these encrusting forms will be found the attached egg cases of numerous species of mollusks and other invertebrates, protected from the swarms of fish that would soon clean off the surface. An overturned coral slab is almost immediately surrounded by fish trying to get at the handy feast.

Another major component of the reef community is the abundant plant life. This varies from the encrusting coralline algae such as *Lithothamnion* and its smaller allies that help to cement the reef together, to the green, brown and red algae that coat over many of the dead coral slabs and rocks or live within the sandy areas between the corals. The most important of the larger algae are the calcareous green halimedas whose jointed plates are formed of calcium carbonate. On their death the plates fall apart and the platelets contribute to the general growth of the reef matrix. Investing the reef on the shoreward side are the ever-present sea grasses, mainly turtle grass, which shoreward of the reef, forms vast meadows, nursery grounds for many fish and invertebrates.

Thus one can see that the reef is composed of many different kinds of life, their numbers far exceeding that of the corals. Most of these species live nowhere else except within the coral community, in a closely entwined common interest group not open to the casual invader.

There are opposing forces within the coral reef, one working to build it up and the other to tear it down. If a coral head is broken open, you are likely to see that it has a number of invaders lying within the coral itself. Several species of bivalve mollusks burrow into both the living and dead coral heads, weakening the stony structure. These burrows are constantly being enlarged and on the death of the original inhabitant become the home of other organisms such as blue-green algae, sponges, echinoids and worms that continue to work on the coral walls. Boring sponges invade the dead coral with their honeycomblike galleries. Boring sea urchins form large holes in the dead coral matrix. Black band disease kills the living coral polyps permitting various kinds of algae and borers to colonize the coral head. Parrotfish nibble on the live coral, a potential source of further breakdown of the colony.

And nature has other forces at her beck and call. Most coral reefs lie in the hurricane and typhoon belts of the world and, like the others, the Florida reefs often suffer from hurricane force winds and waves. These waves strike with such force that they break off large sections of elkhorn coral, wash them across the reef, and tumble them into the reef flat and lagoon, sometimes depositing them several miles from their original site. Even some brain corals can be torn loose and overturned. Some observers seeing a reef after the passage of a hurricane have thought the destruction so severe that the reef could not recover for many years.

But the forces that build up the reef are so strong that the reefs survive despite the dangers. Each day the coral polyps continue to lay down their minute quantities of aragonite, building ever upward and outward, repairing the scars left by the fish, attempting unknowingly to recover the area destroyed by the black band disease, repairing and building up the ramparts that protect the lagoon and the low-lying keys.

4
THE HAMMOCK-
CORAL REEF ECOSYSTEM

The reef tract ecosystem begins on shore with the tropical hardwood hammocks that originally covered all of Key Largo, except for the mangrove fringe. These tropical hammocks are composed of an incredible number of trees, shrubs and plants, most of which are found no farther north than Miami and the hammock islands of the Everglades.

Originally, the key's hammocks had numerous large mahogany and ironwood trees but over the years many of them were cut down for ship and boat building. Almost none of the original hammocks now survive, as much of Key Largo was cleared in the late 1800s for pineapple plantations, lime groves and for growing other fruits and vegetables. The farmers practiced the typical Caribbean clearing and farming techniques, cutting out with axe, and burning, only the smaller trees and shrubs while leaving the large trees to shade the plantings from the intense summer sun. As a result, when land was left fallow, reseeding and regrowth occurred rapidly and after a few years a new hammock appeared.

The old hammocks with their giant mahoganies, gumbo limbos, wild tamarinds, Jamaica dogwoods, poisonwoods and mastics, often have a canopy over 40 feet high. Beneath the canopy and forming part of it are satinleaf, pigeon plum, crabwood, marlberry, wild coffee and many others. The Florida thatch palm is also found there. Butterfly orchids and bromeliads, including Spanish moss, drape the trees while Virginia creepers, greenbriar and wild grape form tangled masses. In clearings moonflowers and morning glories cover the shrubbery.

Typical animal life of the hammocks of North Key Largo includes the giant swallowtail, zebra and julia butterflies and the Schaus swallowtail (now endangered), hammock spiders, the beautiful tree snails such as *Liguus* and the smaller *Drymaeus*. The big blue land crab digs its burrow in the marginal marshy lands and the land hermit crab scuttles about in the dry leaf mold. Several anolid lizards live on the trees, and the eastern gray squirrel is a common sight. More rarely seen is the endangered Key Largo woodrat. Numerous birds make the hammocks their home.

Over 200 species of trees, shrubs, vines and other plants form the Key Largo hammock, but the species of animal life have never been enumerated. Among the plants and animals are over a dozen that are considered endangered, threatened, rare or species of special concern.

The hardwood hammocks protect the soil from erosion and mitigate the temperature within them. The thick humus of decaying vegetation contributes nutrients to the water by means of rain runoff.

Where the hammocks have been scarified and destroyed under the developers' bulldozers, and often lain vacant for years, the soil is washed away into the bordering mangroves. Hammock land is rich with nutrients, but once completely cleared, like the rain forests of tropical America, its nutrients are lost and scrubby growth takes over where for centuries proud trees had spread their leafy boughs.

A unique habitat is slowly disappearing under the developers' ruthless bulldozers and, once destroyed, may take hundreds of years, if ever, to return. What is sad is that the small amount of green space spared by state and county requirements is insufficient in many cases to support the life within it. No studies have been made with regard to the amount of habitat necessary for the survival of the various species.

The keys are surrounded by a fringe of mangroves and buttonwoods, narrow on the seaward side but often present as a dense forest on the shallow, marshy, more protected mainland side. It is there that the endangered American crocodile still survives. The mangrove community is comprised of four species of trees: to seaward the red mangrove, followed by black and white mangroves and on dry land by buttonwoods. Red mangroves with their extensive prop roots are nearly always found to seaward in the water but the others may appear in any order or mixed. Where the mangroves are absent they may be replaced by buttonwoods.

Whatever the succession or order, the prop roots of the red and white mangroves, and the thousands of pneumatophores of the black mangroves, provide a filter for the material washed or carried seaward from the hammocks, trapping the plant detritus along with the leaf litter of the mangroves themselves. In a developed mangrove growth, the leaf litter and plant detritus are broken down by microbial action, primarily by bacteria and fungi. In decomposition, the nutrient enrichment is effected by a loss in carbon content and an increase in nitrogen. About half of the carbon becomes dissolved in seawater where it is taken up into the food web by bacteria to be fed upon by the filter-feeding invertebrates while the other half becomes particulate detritus that is fed upon by detritus feeders such as shrimp. Thus, the mangroves provide a habitat for plant decomposition and transformation into nutrient material for the life of the shallow waters. It is the importance of the mangroves' role in nutrient supply that has resulted in the stringent Florida environmental regulations protecting them.

Where the mangroves have been cleared away, soil erosion may bury mangrove leaf litter, inhibiting the plant transformation, and where runoff carries pesticides and other chemicals from developed areas, they may inhibit or prevent the microbial decomposition of the plant material into its useful state for marine life.

Another important feature of mangroves is the protection the prop roots give to many species of small marine life including the juvenile stages of various fishes and invertebrates. But beyond this, they also offer a special habitat for many animal species that make up the unique mangrove faunal community. Most conspicuous of these is the life growing on the prop roots, composed of tunicates, sponges, barnacles, hydroids, tree oysters, mussels and others. Clinging to the bark and feeding on the algal film are various gastropod mollusks, while mangrove crabs scurry about the trunks and prop roots. The mangrove floor is filled with the burrows of fiddler crabs, often more than several dozen to each square meter. Waving their giant claws threateningly, they serve a purpose much like terrestrial earthworms by overturning the bottom in digging and clearing their burrows. And not the least of the role of the mangroves is the protection they give to the land from the buffeting of storm and hurricane waves.

The bottom immediately bordering the mangroves is usually bare sand or sandy mud. But beyond the shadow of the trees the bottom trends into scattered patches of sea grass that marks the beginning of the extensive meadows covering the bottom across the lagoon and Hawk Channel to the edge of the reef flat. In the Hawk Channel, where the water depth in places may be greater than light can penetrate, sea grasses may be absent.

Three species of sea grasses are found in the shallow waters of the keys: manatee grass, Cuban shoal grass and turtle grass.

While state laws forbid the destruction of any of these three marine grasses, only the turtle grass is known to be truly important to the marine ecosystem in the keys. Manatee and Cuban shoal grass have round or very narrow leaves and weak root systems. They grow best in protected areas of low wave energy. Both are ephemeral, growing in soft sandy bottom and easily washed away by strong waves. Their small blades offer poor attachment surfaces for algae and other marine life and the thinness of their leaf coverage provides little protection for larvae and young of fish and invertebrates. If they persist long enough, however, both may act as pioneers for the settlement and growth of turtle grass, one of the most important shallow marine habitats in Florida waters.

Turtle grass blades are thin and flat, often exceeding 12 inches long and one-quarter to three-quarters of an inch wide or greater. The leaves grow in clusters and form dense meadows that are ideal protection for a multitude of marine life. The blade surfaces increase the attachment surface of a square meter of bottom by as much as a hundredfold or more. The dense root system, in deep sediments, may penetrate over two feet below the bottom and once established prevents further bottom erosion. The flat broad blades offer attachment surfaces for filamentous algae, foraminfera, hydroids, sponges, tunicates, tube worms, bryozoans and hosts of crawling animals. Over 20,000 micromollusks have been taken from one square meter of turtle grass blades in Biscayne Bay.

Indeed, the turtle grass beds contain the richest associated fauna and flora of any known marine habitat. It thus affords a vast food supply for the larvae and young of both fish and invertebrates and, with its leafy refuge, it deserves its reputation as the major nursery ground of the American tropics. It is here that nutrients from the mangroves are mainly utilized. Here is the nursery of the commercial shrimp, the spiny lobster and dozens of familiar fish species including the gray or mangrove snapper, sea trout, barracuda and many species of grunts. But it is more than a nursery ground; it is also the feeding ground of numerous adult fish, including many from the coral reef community.

But turtle grass has another important function. Its long, broad, dense leaves are a natural trap for the sediments carried in the water column.

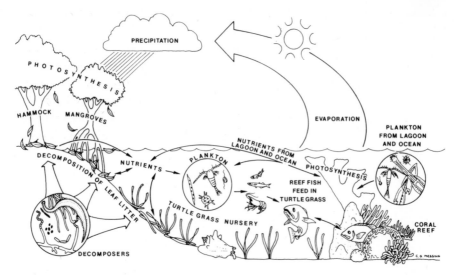

Figure 8. Diagram illustrating the nutrient pathways through the hammock-mangrove-seagrass-coral reef ecosystem. Greatly simplified.

As the sediment-laden waters pass over the grass beds, the sediments slowly sink in among the leaves and eventually to the bottom where they are trapped. Only heavy wave action or the turbulence of boat propellers can draw them back into suspension. It is largely by the role of the turtle grass that water clarity is maintained around the patch reefs, permitting the corals to grow by the aid of their zooxanthellae.

Where water turbidity eliminates or drastically reduces light penetration turtle grass cannot photosynthesize and dies. The loss of the turtle grass through high water turbidity caused by dredging, heavy boat traffic and other human activities may interfere with the operation of the total ecosystem and be disastrous to the adjacent reefs.

The coral reefs and the reef community thus form the seaward end of the hammock-mangrove-turtle grass-coral reef ecosystem (Figure 8). The coral reefs afford needed protection to the turtle grass beds from erosion and heavy sedimentation. The reefs are the home of the adult fish that require the turtle grass meadows as nursery grounds for their young and food for themselves. The turtle grass meadows trap the sediments and clarify the water, enhancing coral growth. The mangroves provide the nutrients for plankton growth on which the coral polyps feed. The hammocks protect the mangroves on their shoreward side and add to the plant detritus trapped in the reduction/decomposition system of the mangroves.

Each is essential to the other and the loss of one affects the operation of all the others throughout the ecosystem.

Once this system and its mechanics are understood, the need for environmental management is clear. If the ecosystem fails, because of human interference, the marine life of the keys may be irrevocably damaged. This could result in the loss of the main attractions of the keys—boating, sport and commercial fishing, diving, underwater photography and the vast support system that is the economic lifeblood of the Florida Keys.

5
MAN AND THE REEFS

Our coral reefs are slowly being destroyed, not by nature and natural enemies but by man and his destructive forces. Evidence of this is becoming ever more clear to those charged with the protection of the reefs and their surrounding waters.

Humans have lived on the keys for two thousand years, having little or no impact on either the land or the sea until the beginning of the 20th century. In 1912 the Overseas Railway Extension opened the keys to the general public. In its construction, from 1905 to 1912, the keys were linked by viaducts and bridges, railroad right-of-ways were cut through the hammocks and roadcrew's quarters were constructed. How much damage was done by the work barges and steamboats cannot be assessed today. But the first of the deluge of construction and land clearing began with the railroad.

In 1935 the Labor Day hurricane struck the keys and demolished long sections of the track and bridges. The railroad was not rebuilt and in 1938 the Overseas Highway was completed and the keys were opened to car traffic. The keys have never been the same since.

Prior to World War II there were few boat basins, or marinas as they are now called, in the keys. Boats were anchored off the shore and dinghies were drawn up on the beach. All this changed in the post-World War boom when developers began the construction of the first large housing developments, each with its marina and dredged channel. Dredge and fill op-

43

erations were extensive and almost hectic in pace. Already irrevocable damage to the marine habitat occurred as mangroves and hammocks were bulldozed away, seawalls constructed, land filled and deep canals cut through submerged lands and across the flats to the navigable waters of the Hawk Channel.

These activities not only destroyed mangroves important to the food chain of the offshore waters but produced increased amounts of milky, cloudy water that persisted for months, resulting from bottom sediments brought up into suspension by the dredging.

Much of the bottom sediments of the Florida Keys are very fine silts of calcium carbonate deposited originally from supersaturated seawater. Composed of fine particles, these silts are easily brought into suspension by waves from only moderately strong winds, as all dwellers in the keys are abundantly aware. In addition to turning the water milky, the silts seed out more fine calcium carbonate particles. It may take several days for the particles in suspension to settle to the bottom and for the water to become clear again. Sometimes stormy weather may keep the water milky for weeks.

The life on the bottom and the corals are adapted to these naturally occurring events. If, however, the water clarity is obscured by turbidity for long periods of time in addition to natural levels, then the life is inhibited and problems occur. This is what happened in the keys with the dredge and fill activities. Coral slabbing and X-ray photography showed that during this time coral growth was almost brought to a halt and did not return to normal until the moratorium on dredge and fill was put into effect.

Turbidity such as that occurring during the 1950s through to the 1970s will not occur again with present restrictions, but water clarity is now being affected by another cause—boat traffic. Every boat running over the shallow waters of the lagoon leaves behind it a wake of milky water where the propeller wash has disturbed the sediments, acting the same as storm waves. An overflight a few years ago showed that the normally clear waters of the lagoon were crossed and recrossed by long milky trails. The larger the boat, the larger the milky wake. The most pronounced were those caused by the dive boats and excursion boats running out of Rock Harbor and the park headquarters. The only waters that were reasonably clear were those around and just inside of the outer reefs where the clear water of the Florida Current swept the sediments away.

But the inner lagoon and the patch reefs, including Grecian Rocks and

Key Largo Dry Rocks, were partially obscured. Turbidity appears to be a permanent situation in the Upper Keys. The former "gin clear" waters are a thing of the past. And the situation will grow worse as more and more boats use the park waters and more marinas are permitted.

Projected new marinas such as Port Bougainville and others along Key Largo were planned to increase boat facilities for upward of 2000 more craft. It is beyond question that the increased turbidity from boat wakes would have a major detrimental effect upon both the coral reefs and the life of the grass beds of the lagoon. The operation of that many boats could well have the same detrimental effect seen during the period of dredge and fill. It cannot be permitted to happen.

The large number of boats using the waters of the Upper Keys or mooring in boat basins and marinas pose another threat. Engine exhaust fumes contain heavy metals and various hydrocarbons and dump them into the seawater. While heavy metals and hydrocarbons have not as yet shown deleterious effects on the corals, they have increased the amount of metals and hydrocarbons in the marine life associated with the reefs. These pollutants are picked up from the water directly by the algae and are introduced into the food chain of both sport and commercial fish and invertebrates. How heavy a load of these pollutants the large number of boats now using the park will eventually deliver and what their effect will be on the marine life is a subject of concern to scientists familiar with the situation.

Another contribution to this problem is direct oil pollution. Very few inboard boats have clean bilges, most have some oil that has dripped from the engine into the bilge as oil drips from your car onto the floor of your garage or carport. Practically everyone has spilled some oil into the bilges when checking oil levels or adding new oil.

Where does this oil eventually wind up? Overboard, pumped out of the bilges by the automatic bilge pump that turns on when the water level in the bilge activates the float. And with the bilge water go the oils from the engine drips and the detergents used to clean the bilges. These pumps work not only when the boat is in use but when the boat is moored to the dock, during the day, at night, day after day, week after week, month after month.

The total amount of oil pumped out of boats in marinas over a year amounts to a small oil spill, but unlike the oil spill, it goes unnoticed. But the oil goes into the environment with the same insidious effects. There is no way to control this as long as boats use the park waters or moor in the marinas along the Upper Keys, but it can be kept within permissible bounds by limiting either the number of boats using park waters, probably not possible, or by preventing the proliferation of boat basins and marinas, which can be done.

Another cause for concern is that, unlike most of Florida, only the marinas of the Anglers Club and the Ocean Reef Club have sewage containment facilities for live-aboard boats. In the other marinas there are no sewage hook-ups and boat sewage goes directly into the marina waters, adding to the pollution problem.

Other dangers from boats and water activities are compounds that leach from certain antifouling bottom paints and are highly toxic to marine animals, as well as creosote from wharf pilings and lobster pots.

Shore developments are nearly always accompanied by marinas with resulting degradation of the environment. But shore developments have other serious effects on the system, among them land scarification, soil erosion, excess land runoff accompanied by fertilizers and pesticides and sewage effluents, all affecting water clarity and quality.

Marinas pose a particularly stressful situation. Not only do they require dredging and bulkheading, they also require exit channels or canals for boat passage. The marinas and canals are natural sediment traps for various kinds of pollutants, and hence sources of continuing contamination. In the keys, the channels are dredged across the grass beds, some for considerable distances before deep water is reached. Traffic through these stir up the sediments which are carried by tidal flow across the grass beds often as far as the reefs. In the large developments, canals are also dredged throughout the site so that each house can front on the water with dock and boat. Thus they become centers of pollution of many kinds, the pollutants continually being released into the lagoon and reefs when stirred up by boat traffic. Their depth usually precludes the growth of seagrass on the bottom and the water is turbid. Granting requests to construct flushing canals leads only to increased degradation of the surrounding waters.

Even without boating problems, housing developments destroy the natural upland vegetation and replace it with macadamized parking lots, lawns and exotic shrubbery. The shrubbery and lawns are alternately sprayed to control garden pests and fertilized to promote growth. The parking areas collect oil residues from cars, including radiator additives, brake fluid, and rubber. Rains flush all of these into the water, including pet feces and many other things, all only too well known to home areas. All end up in the shallow waters, further degrading water quality and affecting the survival of fish and invertebrate larvae and young, inhibiting growth of many and killing yet others. There is no known method that can eliminate water runoff and its accompanying poisons and noxious elements.

Sewage, where humans live, becomes a major problem. No large or small city in coastal Florida has solved the problem of what to do with its sewage and prevent its degredation of coastal waters with its harmful effects on marine life and humans.

In the porous limestone of which the keys are formed, liquids may percolate through as if in a sieve. Septic tank drain fields seep liquid sewage directly into the water in canals and along the shoreline. Cities along the Florida coast give sewage only minimum treatment, if at all, and dispose of it by pumping it out to sea, often with noxious effects. In the Keys this requires sewage lines several miles long running across the lagoon, through the reef and into the Straits, an unacceptable method due to both destruction of the habitats by dredging and the danger of the effluent coming back into the reefs by shoreward-tending currents.

Key developers have now adopted deep-well injection as a method of getting rid of sewage. The wells are drilled from several hundred to several thousand feet depth where the liquid sewage is supposed to be secure and unable to affect the water. No one has proved that deep-well injection in limestone is a safe method. Sewage is one of the most dangerous, infectuous and disease-carrying residues known. It contains untold types of microorganisms, dozens of viruses—most not detectable—and all of the various detergents, cleaners, poisons and other things that go down the drains of toilets, kitchens and laundry rooms.

The deep-well injection method used at Ocean Reef Club at the north end of Key Largo worked so poorly that sewage repeatedly had to be discharged into one of the canals emptying into park waters. The discharge of sewage into the environment cost the club a federal fine in excess of half a million dollars. A deep-well injection system was proposed for Port Bougainville, supposedly large enough to service both it and most other planned communities nearby. While the Port Bougainville project is now defunct, other deep-well injection projects have been proposed in the keys. The danger is real, the effectiveness uncertain, the waters of the park the potential victim.

Pesticides are used freely in Florida and in the keys. Various pesticides are used to control insects on shrubbery, chinch bugs in lawns, and above all to control mosquitoes. The number of mosquitoes in the keys has been somewhat reduced in recent years both by controlling breeding places and by spraying either from trucks or airplanes. Mosquito spray is known to be detrimental to both terrestrial and aquatic life and is no longer used in many areas. Its effect on marine life and particularly on corals is unknown. The amount of pesticides used in the farm land of South Dade was so enormous a few years ago that pesticides formed surface scum on the waters of south Biscayne Bay and killed untold millions of young fish until the practice of washing out the spray tanks and containers in the contributing canals and throwing empty sacks into the canal was stopped by legislation. The practice of washing out the tanks, however, is still continuing, according to reports from the Biscayne National Park, the place most affected by this nefarious and dangerous practice.

During the Mediterranean fruit fly outbreak in south Florida some years ago, spraying for this fly was done from the air, starting at the edge of the beach in Dade and Broward counties. Within a few minutes of the passage of the spray plane the spray was mixed in the surf and killed almost all of the sand fleas, *Emerita*, along the southeast Florida coast. They washed up on the beaches in wide windrows and several years passed before live ones were seen again along the shore where they are the preferred food of pompano and other fish. In Biscayne Bay thousands of young permit, snook and jacks were killed by the spraying. No one knows what effect this kind of spraying might have on the coral reefs where the surf would ensure that the pesticides would be mixed in the water and taken up by the corals, or what effect it might have on the general reef and turtle grass communities.

To the present day, almost all of the extensive environmental restrictions and planning conducted for the proposed land developments on North Key Largo have ignored the waters surrounding the keys. Studies have been made of parking facilities, traffic flow, hurricane evacuation routes, fresh water supplies, so-called green belts amounting to only a few acres among the hundreds of acres of development planned, preservation of the Key Largo woodrat, of the Schaus butterfly, of third-growth tropical hammocks, but not one word of consideration is found concerning the effect of all of the developments on the waters of the park, the life of the lagoon and of the coral reefs.

The freighter WELLWOOD on the reef at Molasses in 1984. The damage to the reef was estimated at $10,000,000 and the case is in federal court. The Molasses Reef Light is directly west of the WELLWOOD at the right of the picture. (John Hallas, Key Largo National Marine Sanctuary).

Boats anchored on Molasses Reef. The fore reef is deeply cut with spurs and grooves among the living coral. The light area curving off into the distance is the reef crest. White splashes along the reef crest are breaking waves. Dark areas to the right are patches of turtle grass. (John Hallas, Key Largo National Marine Sanctuary).

Molasses Reef looking northward with boats moored to Sanctuary mooring buoys placed in lines along the reef. Some dive flags can be seen. (Photo courtesy of the John Pennekamp Coral Reef State Park).

Part of the track through the coral reef caused by the grounding of the freighter MINI LAUREL. The site of the grounding on Molasses Reef can be seen in figure 3 as two long parallel lines on the upper slope of the reef. (John Hallas, Key Largo National Marine Sanctuary).

Head of coral colony of *Montastrea annularis* broken in two by boat keel. (John Hallas, Key Largo National Marine Sanctuary).

Sailing yacht LADY LENA being towed off bank. Note swirls of sediments astern of sloop and behind the towing vessel. The major sediments were stirred up by the sloop's keel. (John Hallas, Key Largo National Marine Sanctuary).

Scientists of the Geological Survey making an acetate tracing of the affected area in order to follow spreading of the disease. (Harold Hudson, U.S. Geological Survey).

Coral bleaching on elkhorn coral *Acropora palmata*. The tissue is not dead but has lost its zooxanthellae over most of the coral. Normal cream color is visible over parts of the coral. (John Hallas, Key Largo National Marine Sanctuary).

Black band disease on the sea plume *Pseudopterogorgia acerosa* at Sand's Key. Dead areas can be seen alongside of some of the black areas on branchlets. (Josh Feingold, University of Miami).

Gorgonians on Bache Shoal, a patch reef, off Elliott Key. Center is a sea whip *Pseudoplexaura* sp. with a sea fan *Gorgonia ventalina* to the left. In middle foreground are sea plumes *Pseudopterogorgia* sp. with a sea fan to the left. (Josh Feingold, University of Miami).

Sea plumes like the one here, *Pseudopterogorgia* sp., grow on the reef crest and upper slopes. With other gorgonians, when set in motion by wave surges, they make the reef appear as if in motion. (Florida Department of Commerce, Division of Tourism).

A diver swims through an outcrop of elkhorn coral, *Acropora palmata*. (Florida Department of Commerce, Division of Tourism).

A stand of elkhorn coral *Acropora palmata* at Molasses Reef showing tumors on the upper surface showing white tissue from lack of zooxanthellae. (Peter Glynn, University of Miami).

A patch of stinging or fire coral *Millepora complanata* almost completely bleached. Normal color can be seen in some areas. The soft coral *Palythoa* in foreground is not affected. (John Hallas, Key Largo National Marine Sanctuary).

A colony of *Montastrea annularis* at Molasses Reef. Formerly bleached, this coral is recovering. (Peter Glynn, University of Miami).

Divers from the University of Miami making counts of organisms inside a meter square in a rubble area. Clipboard with waterproof paper is used for keeping data. Specimen collecting bag is shown at right. (University of Miami).

Corals, sponges and sea fans cover remains of an old wreck. (Florida Department of Commerce, Division of Tourism).

Under a protecting ledge, a dog snapper with yellow fins is accompanied at right by a rock beauty barely seen behind and above the snapper's tail. A blackstriped Spanish grunt is in right foreground and a bluestriped grunt peers out from beneath the snapper, while to the left is a smallmouth grunt. (Florida Department of Commerce, Division of Tourism).

A sea fan, *Gorgonia ventalina*, with its delicate network spread across the current to trap plankton. Various sea whips and sea rods in fore- and background. Bache Shoal, Elliott Key. (Josh Feingold, University of Miami).

6
TOO MANY PEOPLE, NOT ENOUGH REEF

Wherever coral reefs occur, the reefs are deteriorating. Almost without exception, every coral reef whose fame has gone abroad has attracted so many visitors with their scuba gear, cameras and spear guns that the corals are beginning to show the wear and tear that comes from too much human contact. Coral branches are broken; massive brain corals show dead areas where the polyps have been killed by unwary hands or flippers and algae have attached. The worst thing that can happen to a virgin coral reef today is to tell about it in a tour magazine or diving periodical. Reports come in from Tahiti, the Marquesas, Hawaii, the Marianas, Honduras, the Grand Caymans, Virgin islands, Bahamas, Bonaire—the story is the same. The coral reefs no longer appear as they did only a few years ago.

So widespread is the danger and so demanding the diving interests that several years ago the writer was asked to speak to a group considering setting up a marine park to protect an unusual coral area in Florida. After listening to the proponents for a little while, I told them that the worst thing they could do was to make a park of the area because, if they did, they would be ensuring that the corals would be destroyed by drawing attention to them. The area was too small to support the hordes of divers who would immediately be drawn to the reef by the publicity. The proposal was dropped and the corals are growing undisturbed even though close to a large city.

Florida is one of the fastest growing states in the union, already fourth in population and headed for being third, if that is any prize to be coveted. When Biscayne National Park, Pennekamp State Park and the Key Largo National Marine Sanctuary were all first proposed, the question was asked whether it would be possible to have such parks so close to the center of population of the state. It was thought that with proper management and regulations they could survive as oases in the midst of a rapidly degenerating marine system. Many of us had doubts but none of us at the time conceived of the tremendous popularity of scuba diving and snorkeling.

No other marine parks and coral reefs exist anywhere in the world so close to such a crowded region as south Florida and none have attracted the hordes of visitors to such a small reef area as have the Florida Keys. The numbers are mind-boggling.

In 1986 the Pennekamp State Park had 600,000 visitors. Of course, not all of these went out to the reefs but a sizable number did. But in the same year, between Pennekamp State Park and the Key Largo National Marine Sanctuary over 1,500,000 visits were made to the reefs off Key Largo by actual count from boats and airplanes. The Biscayne National Park, with over half of it within Biscayne Bay, is unable to compile data on the number of boats on the reefs. But as this park is the nearest to metropolitan Miami, it has a heavy visitor load and management difficulties. Looe Key National Marine Sanctuary contains only about 238 acres of reef that in 1986 had over 41,000 visitors. It was declared a National Sanctuary in an attempt to save it from the heavy pressures on the corals from thousands of unregulated visitors who were literally destroying it.

This is an astounding number of visitors to these comparatively small areas. If the reefs were strung all along the parks in a continuous series, they might bear the contact somewhat better, but they are not. The coral reefs cover only a small area of each park and the major diving activities are concentrated within relatively small areas, often only a few acres in extent. On weekends and holidays the number of boats on the reefs for diving turn them into small marine cities and the water is alive with divers, sometimes seemingly outnumbering the schools of fish that they have come to see. To make matters worse, many of these boats are either tour boats or boats from diving concessions carrying dozens of divers to be turned loose on the reefs, usually with little or no instruction as to how they should behave toward the corals and their associated animals.

The most popular diving areas, such as Grecian Rocks, Key Largo Dry Rocks, Molasses Reef and Carysfort Reef, show alarming signs of deterioration from human contact. Looe Key is in sad straights, and the reefs of the Biscayne National Park, even closer to Miami, are deteriorating. But what are all of these people doing to the reefs that is causing all of the trouble?

Many of the people who go to the reef own their own boats, are familiar with the reefs, and cause no damage. But a surprising number are completely inexperienced, not only about the reefs but how to run their boats. The result has been a large number of groundings on the reefs, with injuries ranging from only slight propeller gashes in coral heads to extensive destruction of colonies, especially elkhorn and staghorn corals. Reef visitors are not the only culprits, however, as larger vessels also have crashed into the reefs, apparently having missed the channel markers of the Hawk Channel. There were forty boat and ship groundings in 1987 in the Key Largo National Marine Sanctuary alone. One of the worst in recent history was the grounding of the large freighter *Wellwood* in 1984 that caused extensive damage to Molasses Reef.

The commonest damage to the reef corals is by anchor damage. This is due from carelessness and inexperience and a lack of boater education. The usual aim of a boat operator is to try to anchor as close to the reef as possible to avoid having to swim very far to reach the corals. As a result, the anchor is often tossed directly into the reef where it breaks up the coral, drags through the bottom tearing up everything in its way and, in general, wreaks havoc. If the anchor is fastened to the anchor line by a length of chain, the chain itself, working up and down in the surge will crush corals. Unfortunately even some of the dive boats have been seen to damage corals by anchoring in the reef. To help alleviate anchor damage, the parks are now installing moorings at the various reefs so that anchoring is not necessary. This system works so well that moorings are being established in parks as far away as Australia on the Great Barrier Reef.

But the greater amount of coral damage is caused by the swimmers themselves, both snorkelers and scuba divers. Most snorkelers today are inexperienced divers and often poor swimmers. They easily tire and what more convenient place to rest than by standing on a shallow coral head? Each time a foot is set down on a coral head it kills some of the coral polyps. With many visitors repeatedly standing on a shallow coral it is not long before white spotting occurs, caused by the death of the polyps so that the bare coral skeleton is exposed. One would think that scuba divers would not harm corals, but their activites seem now to be more injurious than that of snorkelers. Scuba divers dive to the bottom and slowly swim about among the corals admiring the fish and coral life. They may hold on to corals to take a picture or to pull through a coral maze. Their flippers hit against the corals and may break off branches as they pass through. Some experienced coral reef specialists now believe that scuba divers may be the cause of more damage to the reefs than any other activity. Where spearfishing is permitted, careless use of the spear in inexperienced hands further damges the corals.

It is obvious that swimmer education would be of great importance in protecting our reefs. Every visitor to the reefs should be told of the problems facing the survival of the reefs and how they can help to protect them by proper diving habits. But this is only cosmetics. The real problem is too many people on the reef and this can be controlled only by controlling the population growth on shore by controlling the development of the keys. It is essential that the growth of human populations on the keys be brought to a halt, for every apartment, condominium or private house built means another boat at a dock or marina, and more visits to the reefs for diving or fishing. The reefs cannot stand more contact pressure. There are already too many people and not enough reefs to support them.

7
THE FIGHT TO SAVE THE REEFS

The first major changes in the reef tract started after World War II with increased interests in the reefs. About 1947-48 an enterprising Key Largo resident tried to build an underwater observation tower on Key Largo Dry Rocks, right in the middle of one of the finest stands of elkhorn coral in the keys. Fortunately it was blown over in a hurricane before it was stabilized and the project was dropped for lack of money.

Somewhat later another entrepreneur began construction of a combination gas dock and short-order food store on Triumph Reef. This was halted by a court order and the builder was tried in federal court in what turned out to be the test case for the newly enacted Continental Shelf Act.

Also about this time the first of the treasure hunters in Florida began searching the outer reefs for the remains of Spanish treasure ships. When wrecks were found, the reef over the wreck was excavated, often by dynamiting, and a suction dredge used to remove sand and debris. Parts of the reef suffered severe damage.

Coral collecting became an industry, supplying bleached specimens to the curio stores that then lined U. S. 1 from the Palm Beaches to Key West. Piles of corals and conch shells beside the road advertised the stores. Another type of collecting also threatened the fish life—the mounting interest in salt-water aquariums and tropical marine fish. Tropical fish collecting was particularly harmful as, in catching the fish, many collectors overturned coral rock destroying the protection of many kinds of marine life and exposing to predators the eggs of untold species attached to the undersides of the slabs. Spearfishing, now a national sport, was devastating the larger species of fish such as grouper, snapper, amberjacks and spiny lobsters, among others.

Because of the uniqueness of the reefs of the Upper Keys, when the Everglades National Park was proposed much of Key Largo and the reefs was included within the park boundaries. Opposition to the land acquisition by the park was quickly organized, led by Representative Papy of Key West. The opposition came from two sources, the owners of large tracts of land on Key Largo and Monroe County officials who objected to the land being taken off the county tax roles. The attempt to include part of Key Largo and the reefs was defeated.

A second attempt to include this area within the Everglades National Park was made when parts of the Everglades were added to the park, especially the so-called corridor leading to Everglades City. This attempt also failed.

In June of 1957 the Everglades National Park held a meeting of 52 scientists and forestry specialists at Pine Island in the park to discuss future development of the park under what was called Mission 66. Three scientists from the Institute of Marine Science (now the Rosenstiel School of Marine and Atmospheric Science) of the University of Miami attended to report on needed studies of the marine areas of the park. At the summing up session on the last day, I presented the marine report for the university.

When I ended my report I asked if I could now speak as an individual on an important problem not connected with the Everglades National Park but of major importance to those attending, whose assistance would be needed. I then told them of the destruction and despoiling of the reefs off Key Largo, especially in the vicinity of Key Largo Dry Rocks.

The preceding weekend over 50 boats had been counted on Key Largo Dry Rocks and adjacent reefs loading coral, including a barge with a big crane for hoisting aboard whole massive pieces. When seen, its deck was already heaped high with corals. The same weekend, treasure hunters were dynamiting part of Long Reef in search of wreck remains. On one reef several boats were anchored with their crews collecting tropical fish, forming a line across the reef and turning over every turnable rock or coral slab to scare the small fish out into the open. It was obvious that with this kind of activity increasing weekly there would soon be no corals left. I told the meeting that something must be done, and quickly, to protect the reefs and that the area should be made a park.

Dr. John Henry Davis of the University of Florida immediately made the motion that we ask the governor to make the waters off Key Largo into a state park. It was pointed out that no land should be included to avoid opposition from the upland owners and from Monroe County. Dan Beard, the first superintendent of the Everglades National Park seconded the motion which was passed unanimously. Dan then produced a chart of the Upper Keys on which he, Charles Brookfield, Earl Fry and I defined the borders of the proposed park, the line running along Key Largo to Rodriguez Key, off shore to the channel marker at Molasses Reef, then northward along the 10 fathom curve (60 feet) to off Broad Creek and thence in to the shore. This latter boundary was later changed to run to a buoy somewhat south of Broad Creek to provide limits that could be identified easily and thus be enforceable.

Before the meeting was over, two telegrams were composed and sent out, one to Governor LeRoy Collins and the other to the Secretary of the Interior, requesting action on the motion and giving the names of all of the participants at the meeting. The reason for the dual approach was that both the state of Florida and the federal government owned jurisdiction over the proposed area. The state had rights from the land to three miles offshore. But three miles extended only part way across the Hawk Channel and did not include most of the reefs. From three miles offshore it was federal waters which at that time extended out to the edge of the continental shelf. Here was a problem in diplomacy and bureaucracy. How could two governmental agencies be brought together?

Charles Brookfield, chairman of the Advisory Council for Florida Keys Sites of the Florida Board of Parks and Historic Memorials went to work. First he enlisted the aid of John Pennekamp of the *Miami Herald,* who was a board member. His enthusiastic endorsement brought the *Miami Herald* into the arena. Pennekamp had surveyed the nation's sanctuaries for the U. S. Fish and Wildlife Service and was well-known in Washington. He also gave strong backing to the plan in his widely influential column in the *Miami Herald.* To enlist the federal government, Brookfield and Herb Alley took the Assistant Secretary of the Department of Interior, Ross L. Leffler, out to the reef to show him the corals and explain their importance. Leffler took on the park as a special interest and pushed it through Interior, assisted by Florida Senator Spessard Holland.

In the meantime, Governor Collins switched the reef tract from under

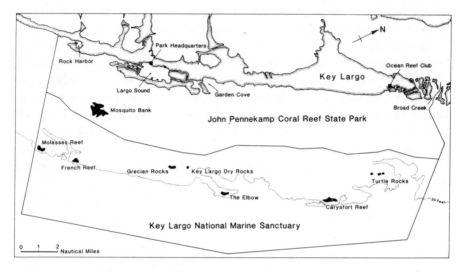

Figure 9. Map of John Pennekamp Coral Reef State Park and the Key Largo National Marine Sanctuary and major reefs. Dotted line is the 30-foot contour.

the Internal Improvement Fund to the state park board. On March 15, 1960, President Dwight Eisenhower, by presidential proclamation, declared the federal waters a national park. The joint action set aside 75 square miles of state and federal waters as a coral reef park. On December 10, 1960, the park was dedicated by Governor Collins as the Pennekamp Coral Reef State Park. Ellison Hardee was appointed the first park superintendent.

To administer the park, a land base was needed. This was provided by an anonymous donor who gave 72 acres to the state for a headquarters. Later the same donors gave an additional 2200 acres that gave the park full control of the two channels from Key Largo Sound into the park waters and included the offshore island. The reefs were saved, or so it was thought.

But the 60-foot depth contour originally proposed was not deep enough. Divers soon found that they could anchor outside of the park boundary, swim inshore and spearfish or collect corals, swim back out and be beyond the park when they climbed back into their boats. Obviously 60 feet was not deep enough.

In 1972 the United States Congress passed the Title Three Marine Protection, Research and Sanctuaries Act, originally proposed to set aside special land areas for wildlife sanctuaries or preserves. But Dr. Dennis O'Connor of the University of Miami Law School thought that Florida should be the first to have a marine sanctuary. In addition, this would extend seaward to the 300-foot-depth contour. At this depth scuba divers could only work with gas mixtures, not simply compressed air.

The petition for a marine sanctuary was introduced and in 1975 the park's federal waters were extended and the federal area was renamed the Key Largo National Marine Sanctuary. The coral reefs were thus protected from coral collectors, spearfishermen and tropical fish collectors. Now the reefs had to be protected from other quarters.

About 1962 an organization called Seadade appeared in the news with a proposal to build an oil refinery and plastics complex on the west shore of Card Sound. To bring the oil to the refinery it proposed to dredge a tanker channel across the reefs, through Broad Creek and across Card Sound. The magnitude of the plan and its effect on the environment raised a furor among environmentalists. James Redford of the Izaak Walton League led the fight against Seadade which was won only after many lengthy hearings and support from part of the news media. While Seadade appeared off and on in the news for some time, its plans for Card Sound were finally squashed when the hiatus between the Biscayne National Park and the Pennekamp State Park was closed.

The nuclear energy power plant of the Florida Power and Light Company then under construction posed another threat to the life of the corals in Biscayne Bay and around Elliott Key. The fossil fuel plant at Turkey Point was already discharging cooling water in the 90° Fahrenheit range and above. The discharge formed a fan of hot water extending out across the bay nearly to Elliott Key. Within this fan or plume of hot water many plants and animals were killed immediately adjacent to the discharge canal, including turtle grass, several species of gorgonians and small corals. Sickened specimens were noted well across the bay. The Florida Power and Light Company refused to believe that heat from their cooling water caused the problem and went ahead with plans to discharge the cooling water from the nuclear generators into the bay which would result in a rise of temperature of about 15°F, which would be lethal to most of the marine animals and plants in the lower bay.

A series of hearings was held at which charges and countercharges were made. The alternative to open discharge was either cooling towers or a series of cooling canals blocked off from the bay. The latter alternative was chosen, the canals dug, and the nuclear generators went on line with no detrimental heat effects on the marine life.

One would have thought that little further activity could occur to threaten the reef environment, but such was not the case. The next threat was from the land developers.

While land development had continued over much of the keys, although at a slower pace, the north end of Key Largo remained as the largest undeveloped area in the keys. Much of North Key Largo was covered by dense tropical hardwood hammock within which several hundred mahogany trees towered above the hammock canopy, some exceeding 200 feet in height. Most of these magnificent large trees were only recently cut down, the largest and oldest by orchid hunters who stripped the orchids from its massive crown and left the fallen giant lying on the hammock floor. The excuse was always that as the land was going to be cleared anyway by the developers, they just got there first. They had some justification for their thoughts.

At the north end of Key Largo, bordering on Card Sound, is the small, old and exclusive Key Largo Anglers Club. On the ocean side, however, is the Ocean Reef Club, consisting of the club and the private homes of its members, a series of canals offering waterfront siting, and a dredged channel to the deeper waters of the Hawk Channel and the ocean. But this was only the beginning. Much of the land was privately owned and the development fever spread. By about 1981 nearly 20,000 units had been proposed by developers for construction on North Key Largo. The largest of these was Garden Cove and Port Bougainville. The latter was planned for 2,809 condominium units, a marina with accommodations for boats of up to 50 feet in length. In addition there was an extensive small boat storage facility and a full service marine repair facility located in Lake Surprise. The total number of boats that could be moored and stored at one time exceeded 800.

This proliferation of development plans raised a furor among environmentalists, conservationists and the citizens in general in northern Monroe County. A series of public hearings was held, appeals made to the state and eventually the two projects were stopped after only a small amount of land had been cleared with the Port Bougainville marina finished but without a channel to the reefs.

Alarm over the keys and their fragile ecosystem caused the state to declare the Florida Keys an Area of Critical Concern and turned the eyes of the nation toward the region. The last page in the saga of the travails of North Key Largo has yet to be written. At present the state has proposed a Habitat Conservation Plan (HCP) that has won the approval of the Audubon Society but few other organizations. This plan proposes seven development nodes, each supposedly with its own marina, in addition to the ten or so existing developments and those in progress. The HCP has other provisions concerning hammock clearing and densities that do not offer the protection of the hammocks demanded by the environmentalists to protect the endangered life.

As this is being written, the state of Florida is in the process of buying the Port Bougainville and Garden Cove complexes from the FDIC which had taken them over from the bankrupt developer and creditor banks. But the HCP still poses a major threat to the reefs and environmentalists are prodding the state to purchase all of the remaining undeveloped area of North Key Largo.

Man's threats to the reef are not over. In 1987 the Department of the Interior announced that it was opening the federal waters of South Florida for oil leasing. State waters are excluded from oil leasing but all federal waters are open to exploration. These include everything beyond the three-mile limit except for the waters of the national monuments and sanctuaries, which are excluded.

Oil drilling along the reef tract presents one of the most hazardous threats to the reef. Not only is there the threat of oil spills but there is the even more dangerous physical damage to the reefs and the shallow grass beds caused by construction of the drilling platforms, the supply and mud boats and the drilling operations themselves.

Even more dangerous than direct oil spills is the long-term effect of the heavy metals and hydrocarbons originating insidiously from the every-day oil residues, often having a worse effect on the environment because it goes on unnoticed.

As there appears to be no buffer zone between potential oil rig sites and the existing park boundaries, it is obvious that if drilling begins, the parks and sanctuaries will suffer. If the citizens of Florida do not rise in protest to this new threat, saving the reefs may be a lost cause. Time is truly running out.

8

PARADISE LOST OR PARADISE REGAINED?

The reefs of the Pennekamp and Biscayne parks have grown over hundreds of thousands of years offshore of a quiet, hardwood-forested and mangrove-fringed line of keys. Key Largo and the small keys and barrier islands extending northward to the mainland were the reefs' protection on the one side and the northward-rushing waters of the Florida Current protected the reefs on the other side. Between these two developed the most extensive and spectacular coral reefs along the United States mainland.

The Gulf Stream, the Great Ocean River, still rushes by unchanged from its wellsprings in the Gulf of Mexico and the Caribbean Sea. But landward, the keys, formerly inhabited only by Indians who lived in harmony with land and sea, have changed with the coming of the white man. Early settlers cleared parts of the land to grow limes, pineapples and vegetables and to build their scattered homesteads. They fished to help support themselves and took conchs and turtles from the shallow waters. They hooked sheepswool, yellow and grass sponges from the clear waters. Times changed, the Upper Keys no longer afforded a livelihood and most of the old homesteads were deserted, overgrown by the hammocks, and few inhabitants were left.

The "Miracle of Miami" took place and the mainland began its transformation into a megalopolis. As more and more thousands of people came to live in Dade County, the growth spread like a cancer over the shores of Biscayne Bay until the lovely hammocks of the keys, the clear waters and colorful coral reefs attracted the newcomers like a magnet. Here was Paradise, only needing the magic touch of men with vision and bulldozers to become the vacation and recreation center for the overcrowded, maddening hustle and bustle, nerve-wracking existence only a few dozen miles away. Man the despoiler eyed the keys with avarice.

Developers, backed by millions from people who had never seen the keys, planned vast housing developments covering nearly the whole undeveloped area of Key Largo, from individual homes to high rises, including boat basins, huge marinas and access canals.

Giant mahogany trees that had seen the coming of the Spaniards were cut down. Giant banyans, gumbo-limbos, mastics, madeiras, paradise trees, stoppers, buttonwoods—all crashed to the ground under chain saws and bulldozers, crushing with them the brightly colored tree snails, killing native orchids and bromeliads, destroying the habitats of rare and endangered wildlife. All were bulldozed together and burned, leaving giant scars in the midst of the green hammocks.

In their places were to be built Port Bougainville, Garden Cove and others, providing homes and apartments for thousands of people, the central attraction a Tropical Paradise of which they would be a part. From these were to go forth a thousand more boats to cover the turquoise waters of the lagoon and reefs, their motors roaring like angry wasps, their propellers leaving cobweblike trails of milky, turbid wakes.

But what had happened to Paradise? It had been lost with the felling of the hammocks, in the smoking piles of debris left by the bulldozers, in the milky waters of the lagoon. Paradise had been turned into macadamized parking lots shimmering in the heat waves of the tropical sun, lost in car exhausts slowly killing the fringing trees, in the oil-sheened waters in marinas and canals, in murky waters no longer attractive to divers and photographers. Only the deep waters of the Gulf Stream rushing past the sickening reefs would remain of the Tropical Paradise and Pennekamp Park and Biscayne Park would be a watery desert. Paradise Lost would remain to show what man had wrought.

For those who think that it cannot happen here, remember that less than a hundred years ago downtown Miami was a tiny village at the mouth of the Miami River and Carl Fisher's Tropical Paradise is now the concrete canyon of Miami Beach.

U. S. 1 from Key Largo to Key West is an eyesore to the weary traveler looking forward to the vacationland of verdant tropical islands and crystal clear waters of the magazine ads. Instead, one meets with garish roadside sign boards and stores and unplanned cluttered buildings devoid of tropical trees and shrubs that could hide the scars of civilization's progress. Only here and there amidst this clutter are glimpses of what the tourist had expected, a little point with waving palm trees, a stretch of open water, a pass between the islands.

Hidden away from sight are the refuse piles and garbage dumps, the excrescence of humanity with no place to accommodate it. The refuse of Key West alone is an unsolved problem. The only solution seems to be to find another unwanted key to bury beneath it. But which will be the next key, and the next?

The city of Key West discharges its untreated sewage barely a mile off shore where it spreads out toward the reefs, causing eutrophication of the surrounding waters. Mounting sewage disposal can soon lead to viral infections of fish as has occurred in Biscayne Bay, off New York and Los Angeles.

Despite the desalinization plant at Key West, most of the keys draw their water from the well fields of Dade County, which itself is having water shortages and water rationing. And for the length of the keys there is only one exit road in cases of emergencies and forced evacuation.

In the face of all of this, Monroe County continues to welcome newcomers; it builds condominiums, marinas and canals that overload the system until they court disaster. And all of these lead, month after month, year after year, to the slow deterioration of the life of the coral-studded waters of the keys that have been the main attraction of the keys and their economy.

If Paradise is to be regained, there needs to be a reordering of priorities. The growth of the keys must be slowed and finally stopped. The scars that blight the roadsides must be covered with native landscape, the buildings remodeled to fit the environment and the building business redirected from new construction to bettering the old. Those who inhabit the keys need to live in peace with nature rather than trying to destroy it.

Perhaps then the keys will again be as attractive to visitors as are the Cayman Islands, the Bahamas or the Virgin Islands. One wonders who conceived the idea to have Port Bougainville developed as a Mediterranean community in the midst of a West Indian setting.

If sensible planning were carried out on the land, the waters of the keys would soon see the effect and the marine life of the reefs and the lagoon would again flourish, for the people of the keys could not live with nature ashore and appreciate their surroundings without coming to the realization of the need to protect their waters.

It is unfortunate that the castoffs of humanity that enter the sea all too often sink to the bottom out of sight. How long would the citizens of the keys permit the outrage of raw sewage in the sea, bilge pump oil, cast-overboard refuse, beer cans and bottles, plastics, old nets and scrap metal, and the like desecrating the reefs if it were to float around in full view? Car owners are arrested for excess fuel emissions and clouds of smoke from faulty engines, but who cares about the long trails of milky water stirred up by passing boats? It is below the surface, it does not get in our eyes, cause tears and choke the lungs. But what does it do to the marine life that has to live in conditions that would be intolerable to humans? If it all caused tumors and lesions and arm rot in humans instead of in the long-suffering fishes, it would soon stop.

Those who make decisions affecting the keys will have to come to a final solution about land development or the keys will become a disaster area seeking federal funds for rescue from economic ruin. But what must be done to have Paradise Regained in the fragile waters that bathe their shores? There are alternatives to the present ruinous situation. Let us seek them.

9
THE ALTERNATIVES

There is no question that the marine life of the Florida Keys is in jeopardy and that the water quality is deteriorating. This can be seen very clearly by the declining numbers of fish along the reefs and the shallow grass beds, and the documented deteriorating health of the coral reefs. The increasing amount of white spotting or dead areas on corals, coral bleaching, the occurrence of black band disease, all speak eloquently—and sadly—of the problem. The loss of most of the longspine black sea urchins several years ago indicates that not only corals are being affected.

Water quality in the keys is affected primarily by factors emanating from the shore: pesticides, fertilizers, sewage, chemical-laden rain runoff, marina pollution, decreased water transparency caused by eutrophication, dredge and fill, land fill and increasing boat traffic.

Physical destruction of the corals is caused by direct contact by humans: boat groundings, anchor damage, spear guns, snorkelers and scuba diver body contact and swim fin contact, to mention only the most prevalent.

The cures for these destructive conditions are self-evident but distasteful. Nonetheless, they are required if the marine life of the keys is to survive. To put the cures into effect will require that local, state and federal officials and administrators face the problems squarely. They must be willing to put their positions on the line and not be swayed by special interest groups and their lobbyists. The situation has gone too far to avoid direct action.

Silly solutions are often thrown out as red herrings when alternatives are discussed. No one is suggesting that traffic to the keys be limited by an access gate at the Monroe County line, that only a limited number of boat trailers be permitted to enter the keys on weekends and holidays, nor that potential new residents be turned away when some mythical quota has been filled.

What is needed first and foremost is a master plan that works and a zoning board to enforce it. Unfortunately, in Florida, master plans and zoning mean little or nothing. Master plans are continually being revised as new pressures are exerted on officials and zoning boards seem set up not to enforce zoning but to supervise changes in zoning by permitting variances. In the critical situation in the keys, this Florida philosophy must be suspended. A master plan must be drawn up and adopted that meets environmental requirements and not the wishes of private land owners and builders. The Florida philosophy that a land owner has the legal right to make the highest profit possible from his or her property must give way to the best use of the property commensurate with the environmental and public welfare.

One of the most important requirements is a moratorium on the construction of marinas or boat basins. Not only are these largely responsible for the increase in boat traffic in the keys but they form concentrations of pollution from which nearby waters are continually degraded. An alternative to marinas for the small development or private owner are small piers extending out to sufficient water depth for small craft. Small piers can be constructed with minimum damage to bottom life and the open board decking offers shade and protection from ultraviolet light that encourages the growth of bottom life. Without new marinas the incentive to construct large housing developments and high rise condominiums will largely end.

No waterfront property owner should be allowed to construct vertical seawalls or retaining walls but should be encouraged to use natural shorelines or use riprap constructed of natural limestone. Vertical seawalls are major causes of nearshore water turbidity because of wave reflection. Riprap dampens wave action and encourages colonization by marine life.

To further reduce bottom damage and sediment disturbance, boats should be held responsible for their wakes. This is already a law in certain navigable waters where boats must slow down to prevent their stern waves from eroding away canal banks or disturbing small boats. In the keys this should be extended to require that no boat should proceed at such a speed that its propellers will create a sediment wake. This law will be difficult to enforce but if all inboard boats are required to use navigation channels from their moorings to the Hawk Channel and deep water and are forbidden to cause a milky wake across grass beds and shallow banks, 90% of all of the sediment disturbance will be eliminated. In some cases modifications to present hulls and propellers may be required. Maximum draft limits should be established for boats using marinas and their channels according to existing depths. In some cases it may be desirable to deepen certain heavily used channels to reduce turbidity from boat wakes. Stiff mandatory fines for failure to use channels and/or creation of milky wakes would soon diminish this source of turbidity.

The main cause of physical damage to the reefs and adjacent areas is from user ignorance and inexperience compounded by carelessness. A strong user education program should be established to inform visitors about what can and cannot be done. This should start with a small, well-illustrated booklet on behavior in park and reef waters, including do's and don't's. Every visitor to the reefs and park waters should be required to have one in his or her possession and be encouraged to read it. They should be made available at marinas, boat ramps, tackle shops and marine supply stores throughout both Dade and Monroe Counties.

To inform visitors, both tourists and residents, of the problems of the reefs and the need for their protection, the county or the state should construct a major visitor's center on Key Largo that contains a teaching museum devoted to the hammock-reef ecosystem, the life cycles and ecological requirements of the major indicator species, the causes of the deterioration of the waters and their life and man's impact upon them. This could function equally well in instruction on hammock ecology, the mangroves and the role of the turtle grass meadows.

The rules and regulations in force at present in the state and national parks are excellent but the personnel and funds to enforce them are limited. Despite the best efforts of the park personnel, the coral reefs are still in trouble, primarily from too many visitors. Various proposals for alleviating the situation have been considered. Among them are the following:

Limit access. This is possibly one of the best alternatives but the most difficult, if not impossible, to enforce. Limited access has long been used in land parks where access roads and entrances are controlled. In our marine parks with entrance possible from all sides, control is nearly impossible, except for those boats using the park facilities.

Rotate reefs. Long considered, this has never been tried. It would involve closing for indefinite periods the heavily impacted reefs such as Molasses, Grecian Rocks and Key Largo Dry Rocks and encouraging the use of other reefs while the closed reefs are given time to recover. The length of time needed for recovery is unknown and the other reefs are small and might not be able to withstand the pressure on them.

Prohibit diving. As the major damage to the reefs is the result of scuba diving and snorkeling, these activities could be prohibited for several years to allow the reefs to recover. Glass bottom boat tours and sportfishing would continue. This would work a hardship on the dive boat operators and dive shops adjacent to the parks but not to those outside of the area.

Restrict diving. It is generally believed by reef experts that scuba diving and snorkeling, particularly the former, cause much of the reef damage. Private scuba diving and snorkeling could be prohibited and diving restricted so that it occurs only from dive boats where the divers could be closely supervised. The effectiveness of such restrictions over a period of time could be evaluated and adjustments made if necessary.

Close the parks. While full closure of the parks for reef visits is a drastic step and should be considered only as a last resort, if other means fail, it may be necessary and it is not without precedence.

While some of the recommendations and alternatives suggested here would result in a public outcry from private citizens and businessmen alike, the situation in the keys is critical and requires strong and immediate action.

The problems of sewage and garbage and trash disposal have not been introduced here, for these can only be solved, along with the problem of inadequate water supply, by strong zoning laws that would slow population growth and eventually bring it to a halt. Perhaps none of the suggestions given here concerning human contact on the reef will alleviate the problem if water quality continues to degrade. The solution of that problem lies on shore and falls within the jurisdiction of the Monroe County Commission and the state of Florida. But for the keys and the reefs, time is truly running out.

APPENDIX: RESEARCH IN PROGRESS ON THE FLORIDA REEF TRACT

The establishment of the state and federal parks and sanctuaries in the Florida Keys created a wide range of management problems. Prior to the Pennekamp Coral Reef State Park, no undersea park had existed and no one knew enough about tropical marine ecosystems to know how to manage them. Terrestrial parks have a long history of research and management, and efficient techniques and methodologies have evolved that, with minor adjustments to locality, can be applied to new parks.

Undersea parks were another matter. The faunas and floras were totally strange and few studies existed for needed reference. Species inventories were needed so that administrators knew what they were dealing with. Even for the most prominent species little was known of their biology and life histories, the size of the populations, their habitat requirements or communities. It was a puzzling situation and there was little money available for research and no trained marine personnel.

The federal government, using its funds sparingly, began to support a series of research programs aimed at determining what it now held in trust. Marine scientists were enlisted into the park service at both state and federal levels. Research, usually by universities and institutions, was initiated under the auspices of the National Park Service, the National Science Foundation, the National Marine Fisheries Service and the U. S. Geological Survey. A broad range of investigations was initiated. The extent of these is too great to be reviewed here.

As the population growth increased in the keys, the pressure on the coral reefs and the whole ecosystem intensified far beyond original projections with the result that the reefs began to show alarming evidence of deterioration. It is the study of these problems that now occupies much of the research on the reefs in attempts to find the reasons for the reef tract degradation and to develop management plans to safeguard the reefs from total destruction.

The information on ongoing research in the keys has been furnished by administrators and scientists directly involved in these problems: James Sanders, Superintendent, Biscayne National Park; Michael White, Superintendent, Key Largo National Marine Sanctuary; Billy Causey, Superintendent, Looe Key National Marine Sanctuary; Dr. Renate Skinner, Pennekamp Coral Reef State Park; Dr. James Bohnsack, National Marine Fisheries Service; Dr. Harold Hudson, U. S. Geological Survey; and Dr. Peter Glynn and Dr. Alina Szmant, Rosenstiel School of Marine and Atmospheric Science, University of Miami.

Corals and Coral Reefs. The concern about the deterioration of the corals in the Florida reef tract has centered research on its possible causes. Basic to this has been the charting of coral reefs and coral patches done in such detail that individual coral heads can be monitored by aerial survey and satellites. This has been a special program of National Oceanographic and Atmospheric Administration (NOAA) itself as well as of cooperating agencies. Along with this are ongoing surveys and monitoring of coral health with relation to the effect of the widespread coral bleaching, white spotting and the spread of black band disease. Drs. Peter Glynn and Alina Szmant and their students are surveying coral damage and disease in both corals and gorgonians on the Florida reefs and comparing this with similar situations in the Caribbean and the eastern Pacific. In biochemical assays they have found Florida corals with low levels of both pesticides and heavy metals, particularly lead, but have not related these to coral deterioration.

Black band disease in corals and gorgonians is widespread and is especially prevalent at Looe Key. There, Dr. Harold Hudson is experimenting with ways to control the amount of infection using a novel method of respirating off the infected areas. One of Glynn's group, Josh Feingold, is studying black band infections in gorgonians, attempting to culture the cyanobacterium and to transmit it to healthy colonies in aquarium studies.

Basic physiological study of corals is being conducted by Dr. Alina Szmant in her research on the relationship of zooxanthellae in the metabolism and nutrition of corals as a means of coping with low and infrequent food availability. Her studies cover a wide range of nutritional adaptations for life in nutrient-poor waters. She and her students are also investigating reproduction periodicity and maturity related to lunar phasing and nutritional resources. Spawning times, variations in fecundity, and size at first reproduction are all data essential to understanding coral biology.

Other aspects of coral growth are being investigated by Dr. Hudson with massive brain corals. These studies help to show the rate of upward growth of the coral reefs themselves in relation to rising sea levels. Related to this are the studies of Dr. Brian Lapointe, Harbor Branch Oceanographic Institution, who is investigating upwellings along the reef slope as a source of nutrients. The U. S. Geological Survey is also assessing the thickness of Holocene sediments and fascies distributions in the reef tract.

Physical Oceanography. A key component of the ecology of corals and coral reefs is water flow across the reefs, either by tidal or wind influences. Richard Curry at Biscayne National Park has been investigating these parameters not only in the reef tract but in relation to pesticide transfer in the canals leading into Biscayne Bay and the bay circulation, tidal currents and flushing rates. Such studies are particularly important in understanding point sources of pollution. Similar current studies are conducted throughout the park and sanctuary areas.

Coral Reef Communities. The richness of the fauna and flora of the reef tract furnishes many opportunities for fish and invertebrate research. To understand the diversity and numbers of life within the reef tract, a wide range of studies is being conducted, including inventories of the species present. Basic to the inventory is the ability to recognize the species, and numerous studies are being conducted leading to the publication of guides and field manuals for the various groups present. At Looe Key these include coelenterates, sponges, worms, crustaceans, echinoderms and fishes. Similar studies are being made in other areas in an attempt to obtain management data.

At the University of Miami, Dr. Michael Schmale is surveying the fish populations of the keys for the incidence of malignant tumors, perhaps indicators of pollution stress or presence of viruses. Mark Eakin is investigating the micro-habitat preferences of juvenile damselfishes in which some seem to prefer live coral habitats and others dead coral rubble.

Dr. James Bohnsack of the National Marine Fisheries Service is engaged in a broad series of studies of coral reef fishes, including research on censusing fish in relation to the ban on spearfishing. An interesting aspect is the changing numbers of prey and predators. As the number of predators increases, there is a decrease in non-predatory fish. It is probable that the changes over the years will show the natural prey/predator ratios as the fish populations reach natural equilibrium. Much interest has been aroused in the effect of artificial reefs on the surrounding natural reef fish populations. Some believe that artificial reefs do not increase the number of fishes in an area but draw fish from other reefs, thus lowering the numbers on those reefs. Research by Dr. William Alevison, Florida Institute of Technology, will do much to settle this question, of special significance when the artificial reef program is growing in importance. Dr. J. Zieman, University of Virginia, is conducting studies of the effect of the grazing of parrotfishes on the surrounding seagrasses of the reef tract.

Pollution. Perhaps the most important investigations in relation to the future of the parks and sanctuaries are those related to the changing conditions in the keys caused by pollution. Water quality monitoring has been done throughout the preserves and is continuing. Monitoring stations have been established and regular water sampling is conducted at specified intervals. Besides the usual water chemistry, the samples are analyzed for heavy metals and hydrocarbons, mostly products of boat exhausts and bilge pumping. Drs. Renate Skinner and Walter Jaap, the latter from the Department of Natural Resources, have been monitoring trace elements and pesticides in both the water and the underlying sediments. At Biscayne National Park the pesticide monitoring is particularly important because of the widespread use of chemicals in the agricultural areas bordering the canals that empty into Biscayne Bay within the park boundaries. Other studies are continuing on the levels of hydrocarbons and pesticides in corals where they may well affect both coral growth and reproduction. Most of these investigations are carried out by park and sanctuary personnel.

Reef Damage. One of the major causes of destruction of the corals and the reefs is from boat groundings. The rangers of all of the parks and sanctuaries keep daily check on these. Many are minor and the perpetrators cannot be identified; these include propeller danage and boats scraping across shallow coral heads. Unless the incident is seen or the craft is disabled, detection is difficult. More serious are groundings by large vessels where assistance is required. Such cases are documented, the amount of damage assessed, the owner hauled into court and fined.

Other types of damage derive primarily from misuse of anchors in coral areas. Anchor damage has been and is extensive. Dr. John Halas, Key Largo National Marine Sanctuary, has made extensive study of the causes of anchor damage and has developed a new type of mooring that eliminates anchor damage. These moorings are being installed over most of the preserves in Florida and some have been used abroad.

Data are also being compiled on the effect of divers on the corals. Monitoring indicates that diver contact may be one of the more important causes of damage to the reefs. In some areas rangers ticket divers seen making contact with coral. Because of the amount of diver damage park managers are considering various methods of protecting the reefs as discussed in the last chapter.

A major setback to the research needed for the study of the park and sanctuary problems is lack of funds. While additional funding would not necessarily solve all the problems in the immediate future, it would allow continuity in research and focusing of investigations on the most important situations where often research is curtailed because of lack of equipment and personnel and lack of political support or concern. Proper funding would allow long-term planning with the assurance that financial support would be available when needed. A concerned and aroused public is needed if the reefs are to be saved.

SELECTED READING

Boling, Rick, 1987.
Reef madness. *The Amicus Journal,* vol. 9, no. 4, pp. 3-7.

Davis, Gary E. 1979.
Anchor damage to a coral reef on the coast of Florida. *Biological Conservation,* vol. 11, pp. 29-34.

Dustan, Phillip, 1977.
Vitality of reef coral populations off Key Largo, Florida: recruitment and mortality. *Environmental Geology,* vol. 2, pp. 51-56.

Dustan, Phillip, 1977.
Besieged reefs of Florida's keys. *Natural History,* vol. 86, no. 4, pp. 73-76.

Griswold, Oliver, 1965.
The Florida Keys and the coral reef. Graywood Press, Miami. 143 pp.

Hoffmeister, John Edward, 1974.
Land from the sea, the geologic story of South Florida. The University of Miami Press, Coral Gables. 143 pp.

Hudson, J. H., E. A. Shinn, R. Halley, and B. Lidz. 1976.
Sclerochronology: a tool for interpreting past environments. *Geology,* vol. 4, pp. 361-364.

Hudson, J. H. 1981.
Growth rates in *Montastraea annularis:* a record of change in the Key Largo Coral Reef Marine Sanctuary, Florida. *Bulletin of Marine Science,* vol. 32, no. 2, pp. 444-459.

Shinn, E. A. 1966.
Coral growth rate, an environmental indicator. *Journal of Paleontology,* vol. 40, no. 2, pp. 233-240.

Skinner, R. and W. Japp, 1984.
Effects of boat traffic and land development on Key Largo's coral reefs and adjacent marine environments. Report to the Governor and Cabinet (Processed), January, 1984. 32 pp.

Smith, F. G. Walton, 1948.
Atlantic reef corals. University of Miami Press, Miami. 112 pp., 41 plates.

Voss, Gilbert L. 1960.
First underseas park. *Sea Frontiers,* vol. 6, no. 2, pp. 87-94.

Voss, Gilbert L. 1973.
Sickness and death in Florida's coral reefs. *Natural History*, vol. 82, no. 7, pp. 40-47.
Voss, Gilbert L. 1976.
Seashore life of Florida and the Caribbean. Banyan Books, Miami. 199 pp.

GLOSSARY

Black band disease - An infection of corals caused by a cyanobacterium, *Phormidium corallyticum*, that eventually leads to the death of the coral.

Calcareous algae - Green algae, such as *Halimeda*, that deposit calcium carbonate in their tissues.

Coralline algae - Red algae that deposit calcium carbonate in their tissues. They are often mistaken for corals.

Deep-well injection - A system of liquid sewage disposal in wells drilled to depths of from 200 to 2000 feet.

Eutrophication - Heavy plankton blooms caused by an excess of nutrients in the water, thus decreasing water clarity.

Flushing canal - Canal constructed to permit dead-end canals or other partially enclosed bodies of water to flush pollutants into the open water.

Gorgonians - Coelenterates with a horny central axis, represented by sea plumes, sea fans and whips.

Halo - Clear sand areas around coral heads or patch reefs, cleared of seagrasses by herbivorous fish and sea urchins.

Hammock - Tropical hardwood forests found in Florida only in the Keys and extreme South Florida.

Heavy metals - Derivatives of petroleum such as lead, cadmium, copper, mercury, etc.

Hydrocarbons - A broad range of petroleum derivatives.

Key - A small to large island in Florida, the Bahamas and the Caribbean. It is derived from the English cay, pronounced key.

Lagoon - The area lying between a line of reefs and the land, deep enough for boat traffic. Used here the same as reef flat.

Nutrients - In sea water consisting of nitrites, nitrates, phosphates and trace elements used by the phytoplankton and from them introduced into the food chain.

Nursery ground - An area where the young of many animals find protection and food during their early growth. In our waters primarily the turtle grass beds of shallow waters.

Outer reefs - The reefs along the edge of the shelf bordered by the Florida Current or Gulf Stream.

Patch reefs - Reef formations behind the outer reefs and usually surrounded by seagrasses.

Photosynthesis - The production of carbohydrates by plants in the presence of chlorophyll and sunlight.

Planula - The larval stage of corals.

Turbidity - Water opacity caused by the presence of materials in suspension such as sediments or phytoplankton blooms.

White spotting - White spots on corals showing bare skeleton and often used as an indication of the death of the coral.

Zooxanthellae - Single-celled algae found in the tissues of corals which assist in coral metabolism and skeletal formation.

INDEX*

*Note: The appendix is not included in index.

Key Largo National Marine Sanctuary, 14, 28, 50-51, 57
Key Largo Sound, 56
Key Largo woodrat, 38, 48

Lagoon, 13, 15, 17-18, 29, 31, 36, 40, 44-48, 62, 64
Land fill, 65
Lithothamnion. See Coralline algae
Looe Key National Marine Sanctuary, 14, 50

Mangroves, 18, 38-41, 44
Mangrove community, 38
Marinas, 15, 43, 45, 46, 52, 58, 59, 62, 63, 65-67
Master plans, 66
Miami, 50, 60, 62
Miami oolite, 19
Millepora alcicornis. See Fire coral
Molasses Reef, 18, 50-51, 55, 68
Monroe County, 54-55, 63, 68
Moratoriums, 27, 45, 66

Nursery ground, 35, 40-41
Nutrients, 25-26, 38-40

Ocean Reef Club, 46-47, 58
Oil
    drilling, 59
    leasing, 59
    pollution, 45-46, 59, 62, 64
    refinery, 57
Outer reefs, 14, 19, 29-31, 44, 53
Overseas Highway, 43
Overseas Railway Extension, 43

Patch (lagoon) reefs, 14, 29-32, 41, 44
Pennekamp Coral Reef State Park, 14, 28, 50, 56-57, 61-62

Pesticides, 39, 46-48, 65
Photosynthesis, 26, 41
Pleistocene reef, 19
Pollutants, 45
Population growth, 49-50, 63
Port Bougainville, 45, 47, 58-59, 62

Reef community, 31-37, 41
Reef fishes, 31-32, 35, 39-41, 45, 47-48
    numbers of, 31, 53-54
Refuse, 63-68

Sanctuaries, 56
Schaus butterfly, 38, 48
Scleractinians, 23
Seadade, 57
Seagrasses, 32, 35, 39, 40
Sea level, 19
Sea walls, 66
Sediments, 26, 34, 40-41, 44, 46
Sewage, 26, 46-47, 63-65, 68
Spearfishing, 52, 54, 56-57
Staghorn coral, 28

Treasure hunters, 53-54
Triumph Reef, 18, 53
Turbidity, 26, 30, 41, 44-45, 66-67
Thalassia testudinum. See Turtle grass
Turtle grass, 29, 35, 40, 41, 57, 62
    turtle grass community, 40, 48

Visitors, number of, 14, 50, 67

Wakes, of boats, 44-45, 62, 66-67
Water supply of keys, 63
Wellwood, grounding of, 51

X-radiography, 23, 25, 44

Zoning variances, 65
Zooxanthellae, 25-26, 41